G. SCHIRMER'S COLLECTION OF OPERA LIBRETTO'S

The BARBER of SEVILLE

A Comic Opera in Three Acts

Music by

Gioacchino Rossini

Libretto by
CESARE STERBINI

English Version by
RUTH and THOMAS MARTIN

Ed. 2484

G. SCHIRMER, *Inc.*

DISTRIBUTED BY

HAL•LEONARD®
CORPORATION
7777 W. BLUEMOUND RD. P.O. BOX 13819 MILWAUKEE, WI 53213

Important Notice

Performances of this opera must be licensed by the publisher.

All rights of any kind with respect to this opera and any parts thereof, including but not limited to stage, radio, television, motion picture, mechanical reproduction, translation, printing, and selling are strictly reserved.

License to perform this work, in whole or in part, whether with instrumental or keyboard accompaniment, must be secured in writing from the Publisher. Terms will be quoted upon request.

Copying of either separate parts or the whole of this work, by hand or by any other process, is unlawful and punishable under the provisions of the U.S.A. Copyright Act.

The use of any copies, including arrangements and orchestrations, other than those issued by the Publisher, is forbidden.

All inquiries should be directed to the Publisher:

G. Schirmer Rental Department
5 Bellvale Road
Chester, NY 10918
(914) 469-2271

THE BARBER OF SEVILLE

Gioacchino Rossini typified the versatile spirit of his age by writing both comedy and serious drama with equal facility. His own tragi-comic life story began on February 29, 1792 in Pesaro, where his father, a local "character," performed a Figaro-like round of duties as slaughterhouse inspector, town crier and sometime republican revolutionary. The mother being a soprano, Gioacchino's parents toured provincial theaters, where the father played horn in orchestras and the boy learned not only horn but viola, piano and voice—making him the only major opera composer besides Gounod to have been a professional singer.

The capstone of his achievement, *Guillaume* (William) *Tell,* was a French grand opera created when he was thirty-seven, after his move to Paris. Though he did not die until age seventy-six, still in Paris, Rossini never wrote another opera after *Guillaume Tell.*

Il Barbiere di Siviglia, a product of Rossini's early twenties, was drawn from one of three satirical plays by Beaumarchais (another, *Le Mariage de Figaro,* having been adapted by Mozart). Rossini had several precursors in setting this subject, the most illustrious being Giovanni Paisiello, whose *Barbiere* is still revived and has been recorded.

At the premiere, at Rome's Argentina Theater on February 20, 1816, accidents onstage coincided with a cabal against the management and partisans of the jealous Paisiello to create an all-out fiasco. Rossini's work quickly rallied, however, and enjoyed success elsewhere. Its first American production took place at New York's Park Theater on May 17, 1819, while the Metropolitan premiere took place early in the new house's first season—on November 23, 1883. Marcella Sembrich sang Rosina, Giuseppe del Puente took the title role and Roberto Stagno played Almaviva.

J.W.F.

Courtesy of Opera News

THE STORY

With his hired band of musicians, Count Almaviva comes at dawn to serenade Rosina outside the house of her guardian Dr. Bartolo, who keeps her a virtual prisoner in the hopes of marrying her himself. When Rosina does not answer him, Almaviva dismisses the musicians and resolves to wait until day so that he may repeat the single glance he has had of her in the Prado. The barber Figaro then arrives and describes his busy life. Figaro promises to help Almaviva win Rosina, reassuring the Count with information that he is in Dr. Bartolo's employ. When the doctor hobbles from the house on an errand, Almaviva sings a second serenade telling Rosina that he is Lindoro, a poor creature who can offer her nothing but love. She passes his test, answering him that she will love him for himself alone, but suddenly she is pulled from the window by a duenna. The barber then suggests that the Count disguise himself as a drunken soldier in order to gain access to the house, and hints that such a capital idea should be rewarded with gold. When Almaviva promises to reward him adequately, Figaro gives the Count his address while the latter reiterates his devotion for Rosina.

Alone in the doctor's drawing room, Rosina dreams of the voice that has touched her heart, although she knows her admirer only as Lindoro and is unaware that he is a nobleman. She leaves at the arrival of Dr. Bartolo and the music master, Basilio. The doctor is worried at Almaviva's addresses to his ward, so he agrees to Basilio's plan to blacken the Count's reputation with Rosina. Figaro, who has overheard the plot, warns Rosina and promises to give her letter to the Count. In vain Bartolo tries to prove that Rosina has been guilty of writing to her lover, but the girl is too smart for him. Furious at Rosina's indifference, Bartolo threatens her with his authority. Later, when Almaviva arrives disguised as a drunken soldier, she manages to hide the answering note which he slips to her. The maid Berta arrives on the scene followed by Basilio and by Figaro, who informs them all that a crowd of townspeople is outside in the street, attracted by the confusion of the scene within. A knock at the door announces the police, who have come to restore order. Convinced that Almaviva is responsible for the uproar, the police sergeant informs him that he is under arrest whereupon the Count reveals his identity to the officer. Almaviva is instantly released; Bartolo is astounded at this turn of events. The act closes with a noisy ensemble of comments on the events of the day as the sergeant orders Basilio's arrest.

In the same room, Bartolo is congratulating himself on finally having gotten rid of the soldier when the Count enters, this time in the disguise of an unctuous music teacher. He pretends to be a pupil of Basilio, who he says is ill. Bartolo brings Rosina in for her lesson. To assure the young people of a moment together Figaro now proposes to shave the doctor, but Bartolo refuses to leave the room. His face is covered with lather when Basilio appears, in perfect health. Persuaded by the Count that he is really ill, Basilio departs accompanied by a farewell sung by all. Bartolo's suspicions are now fully aroused. Berta complains that confusion is driving her mad.

As night falls, a thunderstorm begins. In the midst of it the Count, accompanied by Figaro, climbs through the window to elope with Rosina. At first she refuses to go with them, believing Basilio's slanderous tales about her suitor who, he tells her, wants to sell her to Almaviva. Radiant with happiness, the Count reveals his identity. After a joyous moment they prepare to escape. Figaro discovers, however, that the ladder has been taken from the window and that intruders are coming. When Don Basilio and the Notary appear, prepared to marry Dr. Bartolo and his ward, they are persuaded to marry Rosina to the Count. Bartolo, rushing in too late to stop the wedding, bestows his blessing on the pair.

Courtesy of Opera News

Cast of Characters

COUNT ALMAVIVA . . . . Tenor

DR. BARTOLO, physician, guardian of Rosina . . . . Bass-buffo

ROSINA, ward of Dr. Bartolo . . . . Soprano

FIGARO, barber . . . . Baritone

BASILIO, music master to Rosina . . . . Bass

FIORELLO, servant of Count Almaviva . . . . Baritone

AMBROSIUS, servant of Dr. Bartolo . . . . Bass

BERTA, old housemaid of Dr. Bartolo . . . . Soprano

An Officer . . . . Tenor

An Alcalde or Magistrate, a Notary, Soldiers, Musicians

The scene is laid in Seville

IL BARBIERE DI SIVIGLIA

ATTO PRIMO

SCENA PRIMA

No. 1

Introduzione

Una piazza della città di Siviglia. Il momento dell'azione è sul terminar della notte. A sinistra è la casa di Bartolo, con balcone praticabile, circondata da gelosia, che deve aprirsi e chiudersi — a suo tempo — con chiave. Fiorello, con lanterna nelle mani, introducendo sulla scena vari suonatori di strumenti. Indi il Conte avvolto in un mantello.

FIORELLO

(avanzandosi con cautela)

Piano, pianissimo,
senza parlar,
tutti con me
venite qua.

CORO

Piano, pianissimo,
eccoci qua.

FIORELLO

Venite qua.

CORO

Eccoci qua.

FIORELLO

Piano.

CORO

Piano
Eccoci qua.

FIORELLO

Tutto è silenzio;
nessun qui sta
che i nostri canti
possa turbar.

CONTE *(sottovoce)*

Fiorello...Olà...

FIORELLO

Signor, son qua.

CONTE

Ebben! gli amici?

FIORELLO

Son pronti già.

CONTE

Bravi, bravissimi,
fate silenzio;
piano, pianissimo,
senza parlar.

CORO

Piano, pianissimo,
senza parlar.

FIORELLO

Senza parlar.

CONTE

Piano!

FIORELLO

Venite qua.

CONTE

Piano!

CORO

Sensa parlar.

(I Suonatori accordano gli istrumenti, e il Conte canta accompagnato da essi.)

1

THE BARBER OF SEVILLE

ACT ONE

SCENE ONE

No. 1

Introduction

An open square in Seville; it is nearly dawn. At the left the house of Don Bartolo, with widows having bars and closed blinds which can be unlocked and locked at the proper time. Fiorello, lantern in hand, ushers in a number of musicians who are carrying instruments. Later Count Almaviva, wrapped in a cloak, enters.

FIORELLO

(comes forward cautiously)

One by one, quietly,
Still as a mouse,
Just follow me.
That is the house.

MUSICIANS

Quietly follow him.
Don't make a sound.

FIORELLO

Now gather round.

MUSICIANS

Now gather round.

FIORELLO

That's right.

MUSICIANS

That's right, all gather round.

FIORELLO

Now let me tell you why we are here.
Your benefactor will soon appear.
You'll play the music,
I'll give the key.
The rest is easy, leave it to me.

COUNT *(enters)*

Fiorello, holla!

FIORELLO

At your command.

COUNT

Your friends, where are they?

FIORELLO

Right here at hand.

COUNT

You have done splendidly.
Take your positions.
You will accompany
And I will sing.

MUSICIANS

Piano, pianissimo.
Let us begin.

FIORELLO

Let us begin.

COUNT

Piano!

FIORELLO

It's time to start.

COUNT

Start in.

MUSICIANS

Let us begin.

1

No. 2

Cavatina

CONTE

Ecco, ridente in cielo
spunta la bella aurora,
e tu non sorgi ancora
e puoi dormir così?
Sorgi, mia dolce speme,
vieni, bell'idol mio;
rendi men crudo, oh Dio,
lo stral che mi ferì.
Oh sorte! già veggo
quel caro sembiante:
quest'anima amante
ottenne pietà.
Oh istante d'amore!
Felice momento!
Oh dolce contento
che eguale non ha!

No. 3

Seguito e Stretta dell' Introduzione.

CONTE

Ehi, Fiorello? . . .

FIORELLO

Mio Signore!

CONTE

Di', la vedi?

FIORELLO

Signor, no.

CONTE

Ah ch'è vana ogni speranza!

FIORELLO

Signor Conte, il giorno avanza . . .

CONTE

Ah! che penso! che farò?
Tutto è vano . . . buona gente! . . .

CORO (*sottovoce*)

Mio signor . . .

CONTE

Avanti, avanti.

(*Dà la borsa a Fiorello, il quale distribuisce denari a tutti.*)

Più di suoni,
più di canti
io bisogno
ormai non ho.

FIORELLO

Buona notte
a tutti quanti,
più di voi
che far non so.

(*I Suonatori circondano il Conte ringraziandolo e baciandogli la mano e il vestito. Egli, indispettito per lo strepito che fanno, li va cacciando.*

Lo stesso fa anche Fiorello.)

CORO

Mille grazie mio signore
del favore dell'onore
Ah, di tanta cortesia
obbligati in verità.
Grazie, grazie del favor.
Oh, che incontro fortunato!
È un signor di qualità.

CONTE

Basta, basta, non parlate . . .
Ma non serve, non gridate . . .
Maledetti, andate via!
Ah canaglia, via di qua.
Tutto quanto il vicinato
questo chiasso sveglierà.
Maledetti, via di qua!

FIORELLO

Zitti, zitti . . . che rumore! . . .
Maledetti, andate via . . .
Ah canaglia, via di qua!
Ve', che chiasso indiavolato!
Ah, che rabbia che mi fa!
Maledetti, via di qua!
Via di qua! Via di qua!
(*I suonatori partono.*)

No. 2

Cavatina

COUNT

Gently the dawn is breaking,
Golden and tenderly glowing.
Can you, my love, unknowing,
Dream on in peaceful sleep?

Now that the night is ended,
Waken, my dear and hear me;
Wake to console and cheer me,
Console the pain of love so deep.

Oh hear me, I beg you,
Your fond love calling.
To you alone
I gladly surrender my heart.

Oh enthralling, happy moment!
How I love her!
I adore her!
I'll love her forever
With a love true and tender.
No power shall sever
Or tear us apart,
No force shall tear us apart.

No. 3

Continuation of Introduction

COUNT

Well, Fiorello?

FIORELLO

At your service.

COUNT

Did you see her?

FIORELLO

Not a sign.

COUNT

Ah, I fear that all is hopeless.

FIORELLO

Dearest master, it's almost daylight.

COUNT

I am desp'rate! What shall I do?
Dear musicians, my good people . . .

MUSICIANS

Yes, my lord . . .

COUNT

(*gives his purse to Fiorello, who
distributes money to the musicians*)

I thank you, I thank you.
No more singing, no more playing;
There's no further use in staying.
Be on your way.

FIORELLO

You may go now, no use in staying.
That is all, here is your pay.
You may go now, I dismiss you,
That is all, no more today.

MUSICIANS

(*surrounding the Count, thanking him,
kissing his hands and the hem of his
cloak. He is annoyed by their noisy
demonstrations and tries to chase
them off; so does Fiorello.*)

Thank you, thank you, noble master,
We are grateful for your bounty.

COUNT

Stop it! Stop this riot
And keep quiet!
Noisy devils, you pack of vandals,
Go away!

FIORELLO

Quiet, quiet, stop this riot!
Noisy devils, go away!

MUSICIANS

You have won our admiration
By your large remuneration.
We are grateful, we are grateful,
You have won our high esteem.

COUNT AND FIORELLO

What the devil has beset you?
This is like a dreadful nightmare!
What the devil has beset you?
This is like an awful dream!

MUSICIANS

Oh, how lucky that we met you!
As a patron you are supreme.
We won't easily forget you,
We are grateful in extreme.

(*They finally leave.*)

CONTE

Gente indiscreta!...

FIORELLO

Ah, quasi con quel chiasso importuno
tutto quanto il quartiere han risvegliato.
Alfin sono partiti!

CONTE

(*guardando verso la ringhiera*)

E non si vede!
È inutile sperar.
(*Passeggia riflettendo.*)
(Eppur qui voglio
aspettar di vederla. Ogni mattina
ella su quel balcone
a prender fresco viene sull'aurora.
Proviamo.) Olà, tu ancora
ritirati, Fiorel.

FIORELLO

Vado. Là in fondo
attenderò suoi ordini.

(*Si ritira.*)

CONTE

Con lei se parlar mi riesce,
non voglio testimoni. Che a quest'ora
io tutti i giorni qui vengo per lei
dev'essersi avveduta. Oh, vedi, amore
a un uomo del mio rango
come l'ha fatta bella! Eppure, eppure
oh! dev'essere mia sposa.

(*Si sente da lontano venire Figaro cantando.*)

FIGARO

La la la la la la la la!

CONTE

Chi è mai quest'importuno?...
Lasciamolo passar; sotto quegl' archi,
non veduto, vedrò quanto bisogna;
già l'alba appare e amor non si vergogna.

(*Si nasconde sotto il portico.*)

No. 4

Cavatina

Figaro, con chitarra appesa al collo.

FIGARO

Largo al factotum
della città.
Presto a bottega,
chè l'alba è già.
Ah, che bel vivere,
che bel piacere
per un barbiere
di qualità!
Ah, bravo Figaro!
Bravo, bravissimo!
fortunatissimo
per verità!
Pronto a far tutto,
la notte e il giorno
sempre d'intorno,
in giro sta.
Miglior cuccagna
per un barbiere,
vita più nobile,
no, non si dà.
Rasori e pettini,
lancette e forbici,
al mio comando
tutto qui sta.
V'è la risorsa,
poi, del mestiere
colla donnetta...
col cavaliere...
Ah, che bel vivere,
che bel piacere
per un barbiere
di qualità!
Tutti mi chiedono,
tutti mi vogliono,
donne, ragazzi,
vecchi, fanciulle:
Qua la parrucca...
Presto la barba...
Qua la sanguigna...
Presto il biglietto...
Figaro... Figaro...
Ahimè, che furia!
Ahimè, che folla!
Uno alla volta,
per carità!

COUNT

What noisy fellows!

FIORELLO

The racket they were making was outrageous. They could easily have wakened all of the neighbors. Thank God that they are gone.

COUNT

(looking toward the balcony)

And my beloved, why doesn't she appear?

(walking about and reflecting)

But then it's early. I will wait till I see her. In a little while I know she will appear on the balcony for a breath of fresh air. I'm hopeful. And you, Fiorello, no need for you to stay.

FIORELLO

Yes, sir, I'll go then and wait until you call for me.

(He retires.)

COUNT

That's fine. When I talk to my darling I do not need a witness. She must realize why I come here daily; she must know the reason and feel that I love her. It's curious how love has changed my whole existence. Happiness overcomes me. I wonder, I wonder! Yes, she must become my wife.

FIGARO

(singing behind the scene)

La la la la la la la la la la!

COUNT

Now who is that intruder? I'll wait till he is gone. Under those arches, in the shadow, discreetly, I'll take cover: for it's not shameful to be an ardent lover.

(He hides under the portico.)

No. 4

Cavatina

FIGARO

(behind the scenes)

La la la le ra, lalalala!

(He enters with a guitar.)

I am the barber of Seville,
I am.
I am a man with a way and a will,
I am.

I love the life I lead,
Full of surprises,
When a man rises
Right to the top.
Nature has given me higher ability
By far.

Fortune assigned me its favorite star,
By far.

I'm in a hurry, I cannot linger,
I have a finger in ev'ry pie.
Life is exciting, full of adventure,
There's not a barber as happy as I.

I am respectable,
Highly acceptable,
In any circle I feel at home.
I am reliable,
Clever and pliable,
I am the king of lather and foam.

Then there are matters more confidential,
Delicate errands, secret commissions.
I love the life I lead,
Rare occupation,
What a vocation,
What a career!
I'm needed ev'rywhere,
Wanted by ev'ryone,
Elegant ladies, elderly dandies,
"Make an appointment,"
"Give me some ointment,"
"Hurry and shave me,"
"Carry a message."
Figaro Figaro Figaro Figaro Figaro!
No more, hold on! Have mercy!
I beg you! Do me a favor!
One at a time, not all at once!
Give me a chance!

Figaro! Son qua.
Ehi — Figaro! Son qua.
Figaro qua, Figaro là
Figaro su, Figaro giù.
Pronto prontissimo
son come il fulmine:
sono il factotum
della città.
Ah, bravo Figaro!
bravo, bravissimo;
a te fortuna
non mancherà.

Ah, ah, che bella vita!...
Faticar poco, divertirsi assai,
e in tasca sempre aver qualche doblone,
gran frutto della mia riputazione.
Ecco qua: senza Figaro
non si accasa in Siviglia una ragazza;
a me la vedovella
ricorre pel marito: io colla scusa
del pettine di giorno,
della chitarra col favor la notte,
a tutti onestamente,
non fo per dir, m'adatto a far piacere.
Oh che vita, che vita! Oh che mestiere!
Orsù, presto a bottega...

CONTE *(avanzandosi)*

(È desso, o pur m'inganno?)

FIGARO *(scorgendo il Conte)*

(Chi sarà mai costui?...)

CONTE

(Oh, è lui senz'altro!)
Figaro!...

FIGARO

Mio padrone...
        (riconoscendo il Conte)
Oh, chi veggo!...Eccellenza!...

CONTE

Zitto, zitto, prudenza!
Qui non son conosciuto,
nè vo' farmi conoscere. Per questo
ho le mie gran ragioni.

FIGARO

Intendo, intendo,
la lascio in libertà.

CONTE

No...

FIGARO.

Che serve?

CONTE

No, dico: resta qua;
forse ai disegni miei
non giungi inopportuno...Ma cos-
        petto,
dimmi un po', buona lana,
come ti trovo qua?...poter del
        mondo!
Ti veggo grasso e tondo...

FIGARO

La misera, signore!

CONTE

Ah birbo!

FIGARO

Grazie.

CONTE

Hai messo ancor giudizio?

FIGARO

Oh! e come...Ed ella,
come in Siviglia?...

CONTE

Or te lo spiego. Al prado
vidi un fior di bellezza, una fanciulla,
filia d'un certo medico barbogio
che qua da pochi dì s'è stabilito.
Io, di questa invaghito,
lasciai patria e parenti, e qua men
        venni.
E qui la notte e il giorno
passo girando a que' balconi intorno.

FIGARO

A que' balconi?...un medico?...Oh
        cospetto!
Siete ben fortunato;
sui maccheroni il cacio v'è cascato.

"Figaro!"
What now?
"Hey, Figaro!"
Quite so!
Figaro, here; Figaro, there;
Figaro, yes; Figaro, no.
Figaro, fast; Figaro, slow;
Figaro, come; Figaro, go!
Quick as a thunderbolt,
Bursting with energy,
Eager and willing,
I'm on the spot,
No matter what.
Ah bravo, Figaro, bravo, bravissimo,
You are a wonder, you are a marvel,
You are in luck, your fortune is made.
I am the king of razor and blade,
King of my trade, king of my trade.

Haha, I am a genius! My work is
pleasant, full of excitement, and what
is best of all, it is a gold mine by
virtue of my profitable sideline. It's
like this: if a girl should be in need
of a husband, I go and find her one.
Through me many a widow has
found a second husband. I, as a barber, have access to all houses, with
my guitar as well as comb and scis-
sors. I am a bringer of good tidings,
and so to speak, a messenger of
Cupid. There is no one, but no one,
who can surpass me . . . . But I'd better get to work now.

COUNT (*to himself*).

That fellow, he looks familiar.

FIGARO (*to himself*)

Somebody I don't know yet.

COUNT (*to himself*)

Yes, of course, it's he! (*aloud*)
Figaro!

FIGARO

Your servant . . . O, your lordship!
What an honor!

COUNT

Not "your lordship" in public; in
Seville I'm no count. I have come
here incognito. I'm posing as the
student Lindoro.

FIGARO

I see. An adventure! Then I had
better go.

COUNT

Wait.

FIGARO

Why should I?

COUNT

I'd rather that you stay. You might be
just the right man to further my intentions. Let me ask you first of all,
you old braggart, what are you doing
here? For heaven's sake, you're put-
ting on some weight.

FIGARO

It's from hunger, your lordship.

COUNT

You rascal!

FIGARO

Thank you!

COUNT

In other words, you're thriving?

FIGARO

Yes, I should say so. But you, sir, what
has brought you here?

COUNT

Now I will tell you. One evening in
Madrid on the Prado, I saw a girl,
beautiful, sweet, young daughter of
some doctor who, not long ago,
moved to Seville. It was love at first
sight. I left Madrid and the court,
came to Seville and kept an endless
vigil daily and nightly right here below this balcony.

FIGARO

Below this balcony? A doctor? What a
windfall! All our worries are over,
we are in luck. In fact, we are in
clover!

CONTE

Come?

FIGARO

Certo. Là dentro
io son barbiere, parrucchier, chirurgo,
botanico, spezial, veterinario,
il faccendier di casa.

CONTE

Oh che sorte!...

FIGARO

Non basta. La ragazza
figlia non è del medico. È soltanto
la sua pupilla!

CONTE

Oh che consolazione!

FIGARO

Perciò... Zitto!...

CONTE

Cos'è?

FIGARO

S'apre il balcone.
(Si ritirano sotto il portico.)

ROSINA (dal balcone)

Non è venuto ancor. Forse...

CONTE

Oh, mia vita!
Mio nume! mio tesoro!
Vi veggo alfine, alfine...

ROSINA
(estraendo un biglietto)

Oh, che vergogna!
Vorrei dargli il biglietto...

BARTOLO
(apparendo sul balcone)

Ebben, ragazza?
Il tempo è buono. Cos'è quella carta?

ROSINA

Niente, niente, signor: son le parole
dell'aria dell'INUTIL PRECAU-
ZIONE.

CONTE

Ma brava... dell'INUTIL PRECAU-
ZIONE.

FIGARO

Che furba!

BARTOLO

Cos'è questa INUTIL PRECAU-
ZIONE?

ROSINA

Oh, bella! è il titolo
del nuovo dramma in musica.

BARTOLO

Un dramma! Bella cosa! sarà al solito
un dramma semiserio,
un lungo, malinconico, noioso,
poetico strambotto.
Barbaro gusto! secolo corrotto!

ROSINA
(lasciando cadere il biglietto)

Oh, me meschina! l'aria m'è caduta.
(a Bartolo)
Raccoglietela presto.

BARTOLO

Vado, vado. (Si ritira.)

ROSINA (verso il Conte)

Ps... Ps...

CONTE

T'ho inteso.

ROSINA

Presto.

CONTE

Non temete.
(Raccoglie il foglio.)

BARTOLO (uscendo sulla via)

Son qua.
Dov'è?

COUNT

Really?

FIGARO

Surely. In that house I am the barber, the valet, the surgeon, the pharmacist, masseur, veterinarian, the general factotum.

COUNT

That is perfect.

FIGARO

There's more. Your beloved is not the doctor's daughter. He is only her guardian.

COUNT

Oh, that is even better!

FIGARO

Look out. Careful.

COUNT

What now?

FIGARO

I think I see her.
(*They retire under the portico.*)

ROSINA
(*appearing on the balcony*)

I wonder what has kept him. Maybe . .

COUNT (*to himself*)

O my angel, my goddess, o my treasure, at last I may see you and tell you . . .

ROSINA
(*holding a note in her hand*)

Although it's daring, I will give him my message.

BARTOLO
(*appearing on the balcony*)

What's this, Rosina? Why up so early? And what is that paper?

ROSINA

Oh, it's nothing important, just the words of the aria *The Superfluous Precaution.*

COUNT (*to Figaro*)

I like that: *The Superfluous Precaution.*

FIGARO

Well chosen.

BARTOLO

And what is it, this "Superfluous Precaution?"

ROSINA

Why, sir, it's an opera; it's all the rage now, it's marvelous.

BARTOLO

An opera! Oh, what nonsense! It is probably another of those boring and long-winded musical concoctions, some idiotic rubbish. Don't mention opera! I am against it.

ROSINA
(*drops the paper onto the street*)

Oh, this is awful! Now I've dropped the aria. Would you please go and get it?

BARTOLO

Very gladly.
(*goes into the house*)

ROSINA (*to the Count*)

Pst, pst.

COUNT (*to Rosina*)

I heard you.

ROSINA

Hurry.

COUNT

I have found it.
(*picks up the paper*)

BARTOLO
(*coming out of the house*)

Here I am. Where is it?

ROSINA

Ah, il vento l'ha portata via.
Guardate.

BARTOLO

Io non la veggo.
Eh, signorina, non vorrei... (Cospetto!
Costei m'avesse preso!) In casa, in casa,
animo, su! A chi dico? In casa, presto.

ROSINA

Vado, vado. Che furia!

BARTOLO

Quel balcone
voglio far murare...
Dentro, dico.

ROSINA

Ah, che vita da crepare!

(*Rosina si ritira dal balcone. Bartolo
rientra in casa.*)

CONTE

Povera disgraziata!
Il suo stato infelice
sempre più m'interessa.

FIGARO

Presto, presto:
vediamo cosa scrive.

CONTE

Appunto. Leggi.

FIGARO (*legge il biglietto.*)

"Le vostre assidue premure hanno ec-
citata la mia curiosità. Il mio tutore
è per uscir di casa; appena si sarà
allontanato, procurate con qualche
mezzo ingegnoso d'indicarmi il vostro nome, il vostro stato e le vostre
intenzioni. Io non posso giammai com-
parire al balcone senza l'indivisibile
compagnia del mio tiranno. Siate però
certo tutto è disposta a fare, per
rompere le sue catene, la sventurata
Rosina"

CONTE

Sì, sì, le romperà. Su, dimmi un poco:
che razza d'uomo è questo suo tutore?

FIGARO

È un vecchio indemoniato,
avaro, sospettoso, brontolone;
avrà cent'anni indosso
e vuol fare il galante: indovinate?
per mangiare a Rosina
tutta l'eredità s'è fitto in capo
di volerla sposare. Aiuto!

CONTE

Che?

FIGARO

S'apre la porta.

(*Si ritirano in fretta. Bartolo esce di
casa.*)

BARTOLO

(*parlando verso la porta*)

Fra momenti io torno;
non aprite a nessun. Se Don Basilio
venisse a ricercarmi, che m'aspetti.

(*Chiude la porta di casa.*)

Le mie nozze con lei meglio è affrettare.
Sì, dentr' oggi finir vo' quest'affare.

(*Parte.*)

CONTE

(*fuori con Figaro*)

Dentr'oggi le sue nozze con Rosina!
Ah, vecchio rimbambito!
Ma dimmi or tu: chi è questo Don
Basilio?

FIGARO

È un solenne imbroglion di matrimoni,
un collo torto, un vero disperato,
sempre senza un quattrino...
Già, è maestro di musica;
insegna alla ragazza.

CONTE

Bene, bene;
tutto giova saper.

ROSINA

The wind has carried it away. Keep looking.

BARTOLO

I cannot find it. Why, my fine lady, are you trying . . . (*to himself*) The devil! I think she wants to fool me. (*to Rosina*) Inside now and quickly, do as I say. Get a move on, I said. Go in!

ROSINA

Yes, sir, yes, sir, I am going.

BARTOLO

By tomorrow all the doors must be walled in. Will you go now!

ROSINA

Ah, how dreadful an existence. (*She and Bartolo go inside the house.*)

COUNT

See how they treat my darling! Her unhappy existence makes me all the more ardent.

FIGARO

First of all, sir, let's see what she has written.

COUNT

You're right. Read it.

FIGARO

(*reads: spoken*)

"Your assiduous attentions have aroused my curiosity. My guardian is about to go out. As soon as he is gone, find a way to let me know your name, your profession and your intentions. I can never appear at the balcony without my inevitable tyrant; be assured, however, that every effort will be made to break her chains by the unfortunate Rosina."

COUNT

She will! Rely on me.
(*to Figaro*)
Now you must tell me, what kind of monster is this tyrannical doctor?

FIGARO

His name is Don Bartolo; he's stingy, avaricious and suspicious. As old as Methusaleh, but he still plays the Cupid. Just imagine, in order to get hold of Rosina's ample wealth, he is determined to become her husband . . . One moment.

COUNT

Why?

FIGARO'

He's coming out.

BARTOLO

(*coming out of his house and talking to someone in it*)

Now remember, Ambrosius, don't admit any strangers. But if Don Basilio should come to pay a visit, have him wait.
(*locking the house door*)
If I want to be safe, I'd better hurry . . . Yes, tomorrow Rosina and I shall marry.

(*He leaves.*)

COUNT

Tomorrow he will marry my Rosina! That ugly childish blockhead! But tell me, my friend, who is this Don Basilio?

FIGARO

He's a meddlesome rogue, a shady subject, an eternal beggar. A man without a conscience, as corrupt as can be, and a professor of music, the teacher of Rosina.

COUNT

We might need him; he'll be easy to deal with.

FIGARO

Ora pensate
della bella Rosina
a soddisfar le brame.

CONTE

Il nome mio
non le vo' dir nè il grado; assicurarmi
vo' pria ch'ella ami me, me solo al
    mondo,
non le ricchezze e i titoli
del conte d'Almaviva. Ah, tu potresti . .

FIGARO

Io? no, signore; voi stesso dovete . . .

CONTE

Io stesso? e come?

FIGARO

Zitto. Eccoci a tiro,
osservate: per bacco, non mi sbaglio.
Dietro la gelosia sta la ragazza;
presto, presto all'assalto, niun ci vede.
In una canzonetta,
così, alla buona, il tutto
spiegatele, signor.

CONTE

Una canzone?

FIGARO

Certo. Ecco la chitarra; presto,
andiamo.

CONTE

Ma io . . .

FIGARO

Oh che pazienza!

CONTE

Ebben, proviamo.

No. 5

Canzone

CONTE

Se il mio nome saper voi bramate,
dal mio labbro il mio nome ascoltate.
Io son Lindoro
che fido v'adoro,
che sposa vi bramo,
che a nome vi chiamo,
di voi sempre parlando così
dall'aurora al tramonto del dì.

ROSINA

(dentro la casa)

Segui, o caro; deh, segui così!

FIGARO

Sentite. Ah! che vi pare?

CONTE

Oh, me felice!

FIGARO

Da bravo, a voi, seguite.

CONTE

L'amoroso e sincero Lindoro
non può darvi, mia cara, un tesoro.
Ricco non sono,
ma un core vi dono,
un'anima amante,
che fida e costante
per voi sola sospira così
dall'aurora al tramonto del dì.

ROSINA

L'amorosa sincera Rosina
del suo core Lindo . . .

(Si ritira dal balcone.)

No. 6

Recitativo e Duetto

CONTE

Oh cielo!

FIGARO

Now it's important that we answer the letter of the beautiful Rosina.

COUNT

She must not know yet that I am rich, nor my station. I must be certain that she loves me just for myself, for my sake, sincerely — not for the wealth and nobility of Count Almaviva. You might tell her . . .

FIGARO

I? No, not I. It's you who must do that.

COUNT

You think so? How can I?

FIGARO

Speak softly. I think we're lucky. Look up there; it's just as I have told you. Hiding behind the curtains is your Rosina. Take the bull by the horns, we're alone here. Why don't you serenade her? That is the best way to tell her exactly how you feel.

COUNT

Serenade her?

FIGARO

Yes, sir. Here, take my guitar. Time is flying.

COUNT

I'd rather . . .

FIGARO

Where is your courage?

COUNT

No harm in trying.

No. 5

Canzone

COUNT

If my name your dear heart would discover,
Hear it now from the lips of your lover.
I am Lindoro, who lives to adore you,
Who sees you, admiring,
And calls you, desiring.
Ev'ry whim of your heart I'll obey,
From the dawn to the end of the day.

ROSINA

(from the balcony)

I adore ev'ry word that you say.

FIGARO

(softly to the Count)

You heard it, what did I tell you?

COUNT

I am delirious.

FIGARO

You're lucky, she loves you. Continue.

COUNT

Your devoted and loving Lindoro
Cannot spread many riches before you.
My means are slender,
But I do surrender
A true heart, entreating,
For you ever beating.
I shall love you forever and aye,
From the dawn to the end of the day.

ROSINA

Your sincere and devoted Rosina
Is well disposed toward Lindo . . .
(disappears from the balcony)

No. 6

Recitative and Duet

COUNT

Good heavens!

FIGARO

Nella stanza
convien dir che qualcuno entrato sia.
Ella si è ritirata.

CONTE (*con enfasi*)

Ah cospettone!
Io già deliro... avvampo! ...Oh, ad
  ogni costo
verderla io voglio ... vo' parlarle ...
Ah, tu, tu mi devi aiutar.

FIGARO

Ih, ih, che furia!
Sì, sì, v'aiuterò.

CONTE

Da bravo: entr'oggi
vo' che tu m'introduca in quella casa.
Dimmi, come farai? via! del tuo spirito
vediam qualche prodezza.

FIGARO

Del mio spirito!...
Bene... vedrò... ma in oggi ...

CONTE

Eh via! t'intendo.
Va là, non dubitar; di tue fatiche
largo compenso avrai.

FIGARO

Davver?

CONTE

Parola.

FIGARO

Dunque, oro a discrezione?

CONTE

Oro a bizzeffe.
Animo, via.

FIGARO

Son pronto. Ah, non sapete
i simpatici effetti prodigiosi
che, ad appagare il mio signor
  Lindoro,
produce in me la dolce idea dell'oro.

All'idea di quel metallo
portentoso, onnipossente,
un vulcano la mia mente
incomincia a diventar.

CONTE

Su, vediam di quel metallo
qualche effetto sorprendente,
del vulcan della tua mente
qualche mostro singolar.

FIGARO

Voi dovreste travestirvi,
per esempio ... da soldato.

CONTE

Da soldato?

FIGARO

Sì, signore.

CONTE

Da soldato? e che si fa?

FIGARO

Oggi arriva un reggimento.

CONTE

Sì, è mio amico il colonnello.

FIGARO

Va benon.

CONTE

Ma e poi?

FIGARO

Cospetto!
Dell'alloggio col biglietto
quella porta s'aprirà.
Che ne dite, mio signore?
Non vi par? Non l'ho trovata?

FIGARO

I can guess what made her stop. Someone entered and she got frightened. That's why she left the window.

COUNT (*vehemently*)

Ah, devil take it! I am delirious, I'm frantic! Now more than ever, I'm burning to see her, and to talk to her. And you, you must lend me your help.

FIGARO

My, my, what passion! All right, I'll lend a hand.

COUNT

That's splendid. Then listen: I insist that you lead me to her apartments. Now then, how will you do it? Come, prove your ability and show what you can do.

FIGARO

My ability? Gladly. Let's see . . . however . . .

COUNT

Come on, what is it? Ha ha! I take the hint. Don't you worry! I'll make it worth your while.

FIGARO

You will?

COUNT

I promise.

FIGARO

Then you'll pay me a handsome fee?

COUNT

You'll roll in money. Go to it, presto!

FIGARO

That's different. Why, it's amazing how the mention of money by a certain Mister "Lindoro" promotes my inspiration and stirs my brain to keen imagination.

At the merest thought of money,
That delightful, almighty metal,
Like Vesuvius erupts when it is hot, yes,
My prodigious brain explodes upon the spot, yes.
And my fertile mind is wildly seething,
Bubbling like a kettle when it's teeming, boiling hot!

COUNT

True, that money is a very great incentive.
Now I want to see your brain become inventive,
And devise an absolutely perfect plot.
Let me see how great a talent you have got.

FIGARO

I propose that we disguise you,
For example, as a soldier.

COUNT

As a soldier?

FIGARO

Yes, precisely.

COUNT

As a soldier? What's in your mind?
Tell me more.

FIGARO

All Seville will soon be humming
For a regiment is coming.

COUNT

Right, and my best friend is the colonel.

FIGARO

That will help.

COUNT

How so?

FIGARO

It's simple. By a military order
You'll be quartered in that house.
Are you with me? Do you follow?
Do you see what I am up to?
I'm a genius, I'm a genius, a magician.

CONTE E FIGARO

Che invenzione prelibata!
Bravo, bravo, in verità!
Bella, bella, in verità!

FIGARO

Piano, piano ... un'altra idea!
Veda l'oro cosa fa.
Ubbriaco ... sì, ubbriaco,
mio signor, si fingerà.

CONTE

Ubbriaco?

FIGARO

Sì, signore.

CONTE

Ubbriaco? Ma perchè?

FIGARO

Perchè d'un ch'è poco in sè,

(*imitando moderatamente i moti d'un ubbriaco*)

che dal vino casca già,
il tutor, credete a me,
il tutor si fiderà.

(*a 2*)

Che invenzione prelibata!
Bravo, bravo, in verità!
Bella, bella, in verità!

CONTE

Dunque?

FIGARO

All'opra.

CONTE

Andiamo

FIGARO

Da bravo.

CONTE

Vado ... Oh, il meglio mi scordavo!
Dimmi un po', la tua bottega,
per trovarti, dove sta?

FIGARO

La bottega? Non si sbaglia;
guardi bene; eccola là.

(*additando fra le quinte*)

Numero quindici a mano manca,
quattro gradini, facciata bianca,
cinque parrucche nella vetrina,
sopra un cartello « *Pomata fina* »,
mostra in azzurro alla moderna,
v'è per insegna una lanterna ...
Là senza fallo mi troverà.

CONTE

Ho ben capito ...

FIGARO

Or vada presto.

CONTE

Tu guarda bene ...

FIGARO

Io penso al resto.

CONTE

Di te mi fido ...

FIGARO

Colà l'attendo.

COUNT AND FIGARO

What a genius, what a genius, a
magician.
Bravo, bravo, bravo!
What a brilliant man you are (I am),
That's a very clever plan.
You're (I'm) a wizard,
You're (I'm) a very brilliant man!

(*The Count is about to depart.*)

FIGARO

Easy, easy . . . another brainstorm!
An idea that is worth its weight in
gold.
When you get there, act like a
drunkard
Who has more than he can hold.

COUNT

Like a drunkard?

FIGARO

Like a drunkard.

COUNT

Like a drunkard? Tell me why?

FIGARO
(*imitating the actions of an intoxicated
person*)

If you seem the worse for drink,
Not too steady on your feet,
No one will suspect deceit.
You're a fool who's on a spree.
Even he, the doctor, will trust you.
    You'll see.
Yes, he will, I guarantee.
I'm a genius, I'm a genius, a magician,
    etc. . . .

COUNT

Now then . . .

FIGARO

To battle!

COUNT

On to vict'ry!
(*The Count, about to leave, remembers
something and turns to Figaro.*)
Why, I almost have forgotten,
The most important question!
First of all, where can I find you?
What's your address; where's your
shop?

FIGARO

Where to find me? That is easy.
Round the corner, there is my shop.
(*pointing in the direction of his shop*)
My famous barbershop,
White on the outside;
House number twenty,
Right on the left side.
Wigs in the window,
Quite a selection,
Powders and lotions
For the complexion,
Exquisite potions
Mixed to perfection.
Look for the lantern over the doorway.
There you will find me,
I'll meet you there.
Inside the window
Is my collection,
Cosmetic lotions
Mixed to perfection, etc.

COUNT

I will remember . . .

FIGARO

Better be going.

COUNT

You get the uniform.

FIGARO

All will be ready.

COUNT

You will not fail me?

FIGARO

I gave my promise.

CONTE

Mio caro Figaro...

FIGARO

Intendo, intendo.

CONTE

Porterò meco . . .

FIGARO

La borsa piena.

CONTE

Sì, quel che vuoi, ma il resto poi...

FIGARO

Oh, non si dubiti,
che bene andrà.

CONTE

Ah, che d'amore
la fiamma io sento,
nunzia di giubilo
e di contento!

FIGARO

Delle monete
il suon già sento!
L'oro gia viene,
viene l'argento;
in tasca scende:
eccolo qua.
D'ardore insolito
quest'alma accende
e di mi stesso
maggior mi fa.

CONTE

Ecco propizia
che in sen mi scende;
d'ardore insolito
quest'alma accende
e di me stesso
maggior mi fa.

FIGARO

E di me stesso
maggior mi fa.

(*Figaro entra in casa di Bartolo, il
Conte parte.*)

FIORELLO (*entrando*)

Evviva il mio padrone!
Due ore, fitto in piè, là come un palo
mi fa aspettare e poi...
Mi pianta e se ne va. Corpo di Bacco!
Brutta cosa servir
un padron come questo.
Nobile, giovinotto e innamorato,
questa vita, cospetto, è un gran tor-
mento!
Ah, durarla così non me la sento!

(*Parte.*)

SCENA SECONDA

*Camera nella casa di Don Bartolo. Di
prospetto la finestra con gelosia, come
nella scena prima. Rosina, sola.*

No. 7

Cavatina

ROSINA

Una voce poco fa
qui nel cor mi risuonò;
il mio cor ferito è già,
e Lindor fu che il piagò.
Sì Lindoro mio sarà;
lo giurai, la vincerò.
Il tutor ricuserà,
io l'ingegno aguzzerò.
Alla fin s'accheterà
e contenta io resterò...
Sì, Lindoro mio sarà;
lo giurai, la vincerò.
Io sono docile, son rispettosa,
sono obbediente, dolce, amorosa;
mi lascio reggere, mi fo guidar.

COUNT

My clever Figaro!

FIGARO

I'm honored to serve you.

COUNT

And when I meet you . . .

FIGARO

Purse overflowing . . .

COUNT

Plenty of money and more to follow.

FIGARO

You can depend on me,
I gave my word.
We will succeed, I gave my word.

COUNT

Ah, how love's ardor thrills and excites
    me;
How its sweet ecstasy charms and
    delights me.
Ardor so new to me surges within me,
Sweet is the music of love's reward.

FIGARO

Gold's merry clinking charms and
    delights me.
Sweet is the music of my reward.
Its merry jingle,
How it delights me;
Its merry tingle,
How it excites me!
Money consoles me,
Money allures me mightily,
Money controls me,
And money cures me happily.
Sweet is the music of my reward.

COUNT

Her heart must be mine,
Her love be my reward.
Ardor so new to me
Surges within me.
May Fate benignly
Smile in accord.
And may her favor
Be my reward.

FIGARO

And may his favor

Be my reward.

(*Figaro enters the house of the doctor;
the Count leaves.*)

*FIORELLO (*enters*)

My master is a fine one! Makes me
stand there on my feet for two whole
hours or even longer. And meanwhile
he's roaming all over town. Devil
may take him. It is shameful that I
have to serve such a master — selfish
and egotistic and so in love. I will
leave him for good now. This time
I swear it. This is no life for me, I
cannot bear it!

———

**This recitative is never performed.
The scene closes with the duet of the
Count and Figaro.*

SCENE TWO

*A room in the house of Dr. Bartolo.
The Venetian blinds are closed. Rosina, seated at a writing table, has a
letter in her hand.*

No. 7

Cavatina

ROSINA

You alone have won my heart
With your song not long ago.
As I heard you from afar,
Love was born, I seemed to know.
Yes, Lindoro dear, you are,
You are mine — it shall be so!
Though my tutor will object,
That's no more than I expect.
I'll rely on wit and ruse,
Do exactly as I choose.
Yes, Lindoro dear, you are,
You are mine — it shall be so!
I am so well behaved,
So easygoing,
Always obedient,
Cheerful and knowing.
To guide and manage me
Is never hard.

Ma se mi toccano dov'è il mio debole,
sarò una vipera e cento trappole
prima di cedere farò giocar.

Sì, sì, la vincerò. Potessi almeno
mandargli questa lettera. Ma come?
Di nessun qui mi fido;
il tutore ha cent'occhi... basta, basta;
sigilliamola intanto.

(*Va allo scrittoio e suggella la lettera.*)

Con Figaro, il barbier, dalla finestra
discorrer l'ho veduto più d'un'ora;
Figaro è un galantuomo,
un giovin di buon core...
Chi sa ch'ei non protegga il nostro
   amore!

FIGARO

Oh buon dì, signorina!

ROSINA

Buon giorno, signor Figaro.

FIGARO

Ebbene, che si fa?

ROSINA

Si muor di noia.

FIGARO

Oh diavolo! Possibile!
Una ragazza bella e spiritosa...

ROSINA

Ah, ah, mi fate ridere!
Che mi serve lo spirito,
che giova la bellezza,
se chiusa io sempre sto fra quattro
   mura,
che mi par d'esser proprio in sepoltura?

FIGARO

In sepoltura? oibò!

(*chiamandola a parte*)

Sentite: io voglio...

ROSINA

Ecco il tutor.

FIGARO

Davvero?

ROSINA

Certo, certo; è il suo passo.

FIGARO

Salva, salva; fra poco
ci rivedemo: ho da dirvi qualche cosa.

ROSINA

E ancor io, signor Figaro.

FIGARO

Bravissima.
Vado.

(*Si nasconde, poi tratto tratto si fa
   vedere.*)

ROSINA

Quanto è garbato!

BARTOLO

Ah, disgraziato Figaro,
ah, indegno! ah, maledetto! ah, scel-
   lerato!

ROSINA

(Ecco qua: sempre grida.)

BARTOLO

Ma si può dar di peggio!
Uno spedale ha fatto
di tutta la famiglia
a forza d'oppio, sangue e stranutiglia.
Signorina, il barbiere
lo vedeste?

ROSINA

Perchè?

BARTOLO

Perchè lo vo' sapere.

ROSINA

Forse anch'egli v'adombra?

But if you cross my will,
That is another thing,
Then I can have a viper's sting!
A hundred traps I lay
Until I have my way.
Be on your guard!
A thousand tricks I play
Until I have my way.
Be on your guard!

I know that I will win. But in the meantime, I have to send my note to him. But how? It's a bold undertaking. I am watched ev'ry minute. Never mind; for the present; I'll seal it.

(*goes to the writing table and seals the letter*)

If Figaro would be willing . . . this very morning I noticed him conversing with Lindoro. Figaro is my friend, he's clever and resourceful. He might be just the right man and I can trust him.

FIGARO (*entering*)

How do you do, Miss Rosina?

ROSINA

Good morning, Mister Figaro.

FIGARO

What is it? Why so glum?

ROSINA

I'm in the doldrums.

FIGARO

Ridiculous, impossible! A girl so charming, witty, so full of spirit!

ROSINA

Ha ha! You're making fun of me. What good does it do for me? What good is being witty, with nothing but these walls for an audience? I sometimes would rather be dead and buried.

FIGARO

Be dead and buried? Good Lord!
(*taking her aside*)
Now listen, I've news for you.

ROSINA

I hear some steps.

FIGARO

Who is it?

ROSINA

It's Don Bartolo, I can tell.

FIGARO

Then I'll leave, but afterwards I am returning. I must speak to you in private.

ROSINA

And so must I, Mister Figaro.

FIGARO

We'll talk again later.
(*Figaro hides, but eavesdrops during the following scene.*)

ROSINA

He is delightful!

BARTOLO (*enters excitedly*)

Blast that devil Figaro! The rascal!
Confounded barber! He is so spiteful!

ROSINA (*aside*)

He is screaming, as usual.

BARTOLO

I've never seen the like! My Bertha can't stop sneezing, Ambrocium keeps on yawning. With his narcotics and tonics, Figaro will kill them. Ah, Rosina, you've been talking to the barber?

ROSINA

And why?

BARTOLO

Because I want to know it.

ROSINA

Does it make any diff'rence?

BARTOLO

E perchè no?

ROSINA

Ebben, ve lo dirò. Sì, l'ho veduto,
gli ho parlato, mi piace, m'è simpatico
il suo discorso, il suo gioviale aspetto...
(Crepa di rabbia, vecchio maledetto.)

(*Parte.*)

BARTOLO

Vedete che grazietta!
Più l'amo, e più mi sprezza la briccona.
Certo, certo è il barbiere
che la mette in malizia.
Chi sa cosa le ha detto!
Chi sa! Or lo saprò. Ehi, Berta, Am-
brogio!

BERTA
(*entrando e sternutendo*)

Eccì...

(*Entra Ambrogio, sbadigliando.*)

AMBROGIO

Ah! che comanda?

BARTOLO

Dimmi.

BERTA

Eccì...

BARTOLO

Il barbiere parlato ha con Rosina?

BERTA

Eccì...

BARTOLO

Rispondi almen tu, babbuino!

AMBROGIO (*sbadigliando*)

Ah, ah,

BARTOLO

Che pazienza!

AMBROGIO

Ah, ah,! che sonno!

BARTOLO

Ebben!

BERTA

Venne, ma io...

BARTOLO

Rosina...

AMBROGIO

Ah!

BERTA

Eccì...

BARTOLO

Che serve! Eccoli qua, son mezzo morti.
Andate.

AMBROGIO

Ah!

BERTA

Eccì...

BARTOLO

Eh, il diavolo che vi porti!

(*Berta e Ambrogio partono.*)

No. 8

Recitativo ed Aria

BARTOLO

Ah, Barbiere d'inferno...
Tu me la pagherai... Qua, Don Basilio;
giungete a tempo! Oh! Io voglio,
per forza o per amor, dentro dimani
sposar la mia Rosina. Avete inteso?

BARTOLO

More than you think.

ROSINA

All right, if you must know. Yes, I have seen him, and I've talked to him. I like him and his cheerfulness. I like his manners, his pleasant conversation. (*aside*) That ought to show you, nosy old watchdog! (*She leaves.*)

BARTOLO

Now isn't she a darling! She hates me, but I adore the little rascal. I am certain it's the barber who has turned her against me. Who knows what he has told her! The fiend! But I'll find out. Hey, Bertha! Ambrosius!

BERTHA (*enters, sneezing*)

Kerchoo!

AMROSIUS (*enters, yawning*)

Yaaw! Did you call, sir?

BARTOLO

Tell me . . .

BERTHA (*sneezes*)

Kerchoo!

BARTOLO

Has the barber been talking to Rosina?

BERTHA (*sneezes*)

Kerchoo!

BARTOLO

You heard me, can't you talk? Stop that yawning!

AMBROSIUS (*yawns*)

Yaaw!

BARTOLO

I said stop it!

AMBROSIUS (*yawns*)

Yaaw! I'm tired.

BARTOLO

Speak up!

BERTHA

Yes, sir, he talked to . . .

BARTOLO

Rosina?

AMBROSIUS (*yawns*)

Yaaw!

BERTHA (*sneezes*)

Kerchoo!

AMBROSIUS (*yawns*)

Yaaw!

BERTHA (*sneezes*)

Kerchoo!

BARTOLO

What morons! They are half dead, stupid and lazy. Be off now!

AMBROSIUS (*yawns*)

Yaaw!

BERTHA (*leaves sneezing*)

Kerchoo!

BARTOLO

Confound them, they drive me crazy!

No. 8

Recitative and Aria

BARTOLO

O you fiend of a barber!
I'll make you pay the piper!
(*Don Basilio enters.*)
Ah, Don Basilio! Timely arrival!
Listen: tomorrow and not a moment later, I have decided to marry my Rosina. You understand me?

BASILIO (*dopo molte riverenze*)

Eh, voi dite benissimo
e appunto io qui veniva ad avvisarvi...

(*chiamandolo a parte*)

Ma segretezza! È giunto
il Conte d'Almaviva.

BARTOLO

Chi? L'incognito amante
della Rosina?

BASILIO

Appunto quello.

BARTOLO

Oh diavolo!
Ah, qui ci vuol rimedio!

BASILIO

Certo; ma... alla sordina.

BARTOLO

Sarebbe a dir?

BASILIO

Così, con buona grazia
bisogna principiare
a inventar qualche favola
che al pubblico lo metta in mala vista,
che comparir lo faccia
un uomo infame, un'anima perduta...
Io, io vi servirò: fra quattro giorni,
credete a me, Basilio ve lo giura,
noi lo farem sloggiar da queste mura.

BARTOLO

E voi credete?

BASILIO

Oh certo! È il mio sistema.
E non sbaglia.

BARTOLO

E vorreste?
Ma una calunnia...

BASILIO

Ah, dunque
la calunnia cos'è voi non sapete?

BARTOLO

No, davvero.

BASILIO

No? Uditemi e tacete.

La calunnia è un venticello,
un'auretta assai gentile
che insensibile, sottile,
leggermente, dolcemente,
incomincia a sussurrar.
Piano piano, terra terra,
sottovoce, sibilando;
va scorrendo, va ronzando;
nell' orecchie della gente
s'introduce destramente,
e le teste ed i cervelli
fa stordire e fa gonfiar.
Dalla bocca fuori uscendo
lo schiamazzo va crescendo,
prende forza a poco a poco,
vola già di loco in loco;
sembra il tuono, la tempesta
che nel sen della foresta
va fischiando, brontolando
e ti fa d'orror gelar.
Alla fin trabocca e scoppia,
si propaga, si raddoppia
e produce un'esplosione
come un colpo di cannone,
un tremuoto, un temporale,
un tumulto generale,
che fa l'aria rimbombar.
E il meschino calunniato,
avvilito, calpestato,
sotto il pubblico flagello
per gran sorte va a crepar.

Ah! che ne dite?

BARTOLO

Eh! sarà ver, ma intanto
si perde tempo e qui stringe il bisogno.
No: vo' fare a modo mio:
in mia camera andiam. Voglio che
    insieme
il contratto di nozze ora stendiamo.
Quando sarà mia moglie,
da questi zerbinotti innamorati
metterla in salvo sarà pensier mio.

BASILIO

(*bowing very low*)

You're absolutely right, my friend. I came to bring you news of great importance (*taking him aside*) but . . . sotto voce! Now guess who has arrived in town?

BARTOLO

Who? Not Almaviva, Rosina's suitor?

BASILIO

Count Almaviva.

BARTOLO

How terrible! That calls for quick action.

BASILIO

Presto! But . . . con sordino.

BARTOLO

What do you mean?

BASILIO

I mean that very subtly one must invent a falsehood which will blacken his character, discredit him, and spoil his reputation. Damage him so completely, cause such a scandal, he'll be disgraced forever. And I'm the man to do it. Before you know it . . . just take my word . . . as sure as I'm Basilio, we'll chase him out of town, make him an outcast!

BARTOLO

You really think so?

BASILIO

I know so. I have a method and it's foolproof.

BARTOLO

Is it really? But that would be slander!

BASILIO

Dear doctor, as the means to an end, one can condone it.

BARTOLO

Well, how would you?

BASILIO

How? Sit quietly, while I propone it.

Let me teach you the art of slander,
So ethereal you scarcely feel it.
Not a motion will reveal it,
Till it gently, o so gently,
Almost imperceptibly begins to grow.
First a murmur, slowly seeping,
Then a whisper, lowly creeping,
Slyly sneaking, softly sliding,
Faintly humming, smoothly gliding.
Then it suddenly commences,
Coming nearer, reaching people's ears
    and senses.
First a mere insinuation,
Just a hinted accusation,
Slowly growing to a rumor
Which will shortly start to flow.
What began as innuendo
Soon is swelling in crescendo;
Gossip turning into scandal,
Stopping nowhere, hard to handle;
Louder, bolder, brazen sounding,
Stomping, beating, thumping, pound-
    ing,
Shrieking, banging, booming, clanging,
Spreading horror through the air.
Rising higher, overflowing,
Whipped to fury, madly growing,
Like a stream of lava pouring,
Like a mighty cannon roaring.
A tremendous tempest raking,
A tornado splitting, shaking,
Like the day of judgment breaking,
Pandemonium ev'rywhere!
And the victim, poor accused one,
Wretched, slandered and abused one,
Has to slink away in shame
And wish he never had been born.

Well, do you like it?

BARTOLO

Yes, it's not bad. But meanwhile we're losing time and the matter is urgent. No, we'd better do it my way. I will marry her at once. This very minute let us go to my study and write the contract. Once we are safely married, these juvenile affairs and peccadillos with would-be lovers will soon be forgotten.

BASILIO

(Vengan danari: al resto son qua io.)
(*Entrano nella prima camera a destra.*)

No. 9

Recitativo ed Aria

FIGARO

Ma bravi! ma benone!
Ho inteso tutto. Evviva il buon Dottore.
Povero babbuino!
Tua sposa? Eh via! Pulisciti il boc-
chino.
Or che stanno là chiusi
procuriam di parlare alla ragazza:
eccola appunto.

ROSINA (*entrando*)

Ebbene, signor Figaro?

FIGARO

Gran cose, signorina.

ROSINA

Sì, davvero?

FIGARO

Mangerem dei confetti.

ROSINA

Come sarebbe a dir?

FIGARO

Sarebbe a dire
che il vostro bel tutore ha stabilito
esser dentro doman vostro marito.

ROSINA

Eh, via!

FIGARO

Oh, ve lo giuro;
a stender il contratto
col maestro di musica
là dentro s'è serrato.

ROSINA

Sì? oh, l'ha sbagliata affè!
Povero sciocco! L'avrà da a far con me.
Ma dite, signor Figaro,
voi poco fa sotto le mie finestre
parlavate a un signore . . .

FIGARO

Ah, un mio cugino,
un bravo giovinotto; buona testa,
ottimo cuor; qui venne
i suoi studi a compire,
e il poverin cerca di far fortuna.

ROSINA

Fortuna? eh, la farà.

FIGARO

Oh, ne dubito assai: in confidenza
ha un gran difetto addosso.

ROSINA

Un gran difetto?

FIGARO

Ah, grande:
è innamorato morto.

ROSINA

Sì, davvero?
Quel giovane, vedete,
m'interessa moltissimo.

FIGARO

Per bacco!

ROSINA

Non ci credete?

FIGARO

Oh sì!

ROSINA

E la sua bella,
dite, abita lontano?

FIGARO

Oh no! . . . cioè . . .
Qui! . . . due passi . . .

BASILIO (*aside*)

I smell a profit. It's rotten, but what of it?

(*They enter Bartolo's study.*)

No. 9

Recitative and Duet

FIGARO

(*coming forward cautiously*)

So that's it! Now I know what they are up to. A wizard of a doctor! Marry the girl for her money! Is that it? You wait. We'll teach you a lesson. While they're plotting and scheming, I must talk to Rosina and warn her. I see her coming.

ROSINA (*entering*)

What news, Mister Figaro?

FIGARO

Just wait until you hear it!

ROSINA

Well, what is it?

FIGARO

We'll be having a picnic!

ROSINA

What do you mean by that?

FIGARO

It's very simple. By tomorrow your worthy guardian has arranged to become your worthy husband.

ROSINA

You're joking!

FIGARO

Oh, no, I'm serious! There in the doctor's study, he himself and Basilio are drawing up the contract.

ROSINA

Are they? How silly can they be? Have they forgotten they'll have to deal with me? But tell me, Mister Figaro, not long ago there beneath my window, you were talking to someone . . .

FIGARO

Oh, that was my cousin, a promising young fellow. He has talent, a heart of gold; he's living in Seville as a student. And the poor boy hopes that he'll be successful.

ROSINA

Successful? That he will be!

FIGARO

Oh, I'm not quite so certain; and to be truthful, he has a dreadful weakness.

ROSINA

A dreadful weakness?

FIGARO

Yes, dreadful. He's head over heels in love.

ROSINA

Oh, is he really? In confidence . . . this student . . . I'm most anxious to talk to him.

FIGARO

You don't say.

ROSINA

Don't you believe me?

FIGARO

I do.

ROSINA

And his beloved . . . tell me, does she live nearby?

FIGARO

She does. Let me see . . . yes, in this house.

ROSINA

Ma è bella?

FIGARO

Oh, bella assai!
Eccovi il suo ritratto in due parole:
grassotta, genialotta,
capello nero, guancia porporina,
occhio che parla, mano che
    innamora . . .

ROSINA

E il nome?

FIGARO

Ah, il nome ancora?
Il nome . . . Ah, che bel nome!
Si chiama . . .

ROSINA

Ebben, si chiama?

FIGARO

Poverina! . . .
Si chiama r . . . o . . . ro . . . s . . . i . . .
si . . . rosi . . . n . . . a . . . na . . .
Rosina.

ROSINA

Dunque io son . . . tu non m'inganni?
Dunque io son la fortunata!
(Già me l'ero immaginata:
lo sapevo pria di te.)

FIGARO

Di Lindoro il vago oggetto
siete voi, bella Rosina.
(Oh, che volpe sopraffina,
ma l'avrà da far con me.)

ROSINA

Senti, senti . . . ma a Lindoro
per parlar come si fa?

FIGARO

Zitto, zitto, qui Lindoro
per parlarvi or or sarà

ROSINA

Per parlarmi? Bravo! bravo!
Venga pur, ma con prudenza;
io già moro d'impazienza!
Ma che tarda? ma che fa?

FIGARO

Egli attende qualche segno,
poverin, del vostro affetto;
sol due righe di biglietto
gli mandate, e qui verrà.
Che ne dite?

ROSINA

Non vorrei . . .

FIGARO

Su, coraggio.

ROSINA

Non saprei . . .

FIGARO

Sol due righe . . .

ROSINA

Mi vergogno . . .

FIGARO

Ma di che? di che? si sa!
    (*andando allo scrittoio*)
Presto, presto; qua il biglietto.

ROSINA

(*richiamandolo, cava dalla tasca il biglietto e glielo dà.*)
Un biglietto? . . . eccolo qua.

FIGARO (*attonito*)

Già era scritto? Ve', che bestia!
Il maestro faccio a lei!

ROSINA

Fortunati affeti miei!
Io comincio a respirar.

FIGARO

Ah, che in cattedra costei di malizia
    può dettar.

ROSINA

Ah, tu solo, amor, tu sei che mi devi
    consolar!

ROSINA

Is she pretty?

FIGARO

She is a beauty. Here is a brief descrip-
tion of what she looks like. Her figure
like a Venus, her hair like velvet,
cheeks like two roses, her eyes are
sparkling, peach-like complexion.

ROSINA

And her name?

FIGARO

I have forgotten. One moment . . . it's
coming back now. Her name is—

ROSINA

Go on, what is it?

FIGARO

You'll never guess it! I'll spell it. R O,
Ro, S I, Rosi, N A, Rosina!

ROSINA

I'm his love. . . . you really mean it?
I myself am his beloved!
I confess I had foreseen it,
I admit I always knew.

FIGARO

You're the goal of his affection,
You alone, my dear Rosina.
He adores you, lovely Rosina.
(aside)
You are clever, signorina.
But then I am clever too.

ROSINA

Let me ask you. Will Lindoro come
to see me,
Would you say?

FIGARO

Do not worry, your Lindoro wants to
see you right away.

ROSINA

How exciting! Let him come here,
But with caution and discreetly.
I'm so happy, yes, so very happy!
But what's causing his delay?

FIGARO

He is waiting for permission,
For a sign that you invite him.
Just a tiny written message,
Just a line of your approval,
And he'll visit you today.
You will see him this very day.
Will you do it?

ROSINA (pretending)

No, I cannot.

FIGARO

Don't be bashful.

ROSINA (pretending)

I don't dare to.

FIGARO

It's so easy.

ROSINA (pretending)

I'm embarrassed.

FIGARO

Why on earth? Tell me why?
Say why? (going to the writingtable)
Waste no time and write the letter.

ROSINA

(takes the letter from her pocket and
gives it to him)

It so happens that it is done.

FIGARO

(taken aback)

So, she's embarrassed! Am I stupid,
what an idiot I have been!

ROSINA

Now my happy heart beats faster,
I am overcome with joy.

FIGARO

I admit she is my master,
While she looks so sweet and coy.

ROSINA

Love shall be my inspiration,
My delight, my shining star.

FIGARO

Donne, donne, eterni Dei,
  chi v'arriva a indovinar?

ROSINA

Senti, senti, ma Lindoro . . .

FIGARO

Qui verrà! A momenti
  per parlarvi qui sarà.

ROSINA

Venga pur, ma con prudenza.

FIGARO

Zitto, zitto, qui verrà.

ROSINA

Ah, tu solo, amor, tu sei
che mi devi consolar!

FIGARO

Donne, donne, eterni Dei
chi v'arriva a indovinar
a indovinar!

(*Figaro parte.*)

No. 10

Recitativo ed Aria

ROSINA

Ora mi sento meglio. Questo Figaro
è un bravo giovinotto.

BARTOLO (*entrando*)

Insomma, colle buone,
potrei sapere dalla mia Rosina
che venne a far colui questa mattina?

ROSINA

Figaro? Non so nulla.

BARTOLO

Ti parlò?

ROSINA

Mi parlò.

BARTOLO

Che ti diceva?

ROSINA

Oh! mi parlò di certe bagattelle,
Del figurin di Francia,
del mal della sua figlia Marcellina.

BARTOLO

Davvero! Ed io scommetto . . .
che portò la risposta al tuo biglietto.

ROSINA

Qual biglietto?

BARTOLO

Che serve!
L'arietta dell'INUTIL PRECAU-
  ZIONE
che ti cadde staman giù dal balcone.
Vi fate rossa? (Avessi indovinato!)
Che vuol dir questo dito
così sporco d'inchiostro?

ROSINA

Sporco? oh, nulla.
Io me l'avea scottato,
e coll'inchiostro or or l'ho medicato.

BARTOLO

(Diavolo!) E questi fogli.
Or son cinque . . . eran sei.

ROSINA

Que' fogli? . . . è vero.
D'uno mi son servita
a mandar dei confetti a Marcellina.

BARTOLO

Bravissima! E la penna
perchè fu temperata?

ROSINA

(Maledetto!) La penna! . . .
Per disegnare un fiore sul tamburo.

FIGARO

Women baffle all creation,
What a puzzle women are!

ROSINA

Are you certain that Lindoro . . .

FIGARO

Yes, I am. I have told you
He's already on his way.

ROSINA

But with caution and discreetly . . .

FIGARO

He's already on his way.

ROSINA

Love shall be my inspiration,
My delight, my shining star.

FIGARO

Women baffle all creation,
What a puzzle women are!
Too sly by far!
(*Figaro leaves.*)

No. 10

Recitative and Aria

ROSINA

Now I feel so much better. Thanks to
Figaro, my note will be delivered.

BARTOLO

(*enters from his study*)

Rosina, don't be sulky; be a good girl
now, tell me, just between us, what
did the barber say to you this morning?

ROSINA

Figaro? Nothing special.

BARTOLO

He was here?

ROSINA

Yes, he was.

BARTOLO

What did he tell you?

ROSINA

Oh, nothing much. We talked about
the weather, of a new Paris hairstyle,
the headache of his cousin Marcellina.

BARTOLO

How touching! And I will wager that
he brought you an answer to a certain message.

ROSINA

To a message?

BARTOLO

Exactly. That paper with the words
to that aria which you dropped to
the street this very morning. Look
how you're blushing. (*aside*) I think
this time I've caught her. (*aloud*)
Tell me, why is your finger all covered with ink spots?

ROSINA

Ink spots? Oh, is it? Oh, I had burned
my finger, and when it hurt me, I
dipped it into the ink well.

BARTOLO

(*aside*) Hang it all! (*aloud*) But these
papers . . . I see six here, there were
seven.

ROSINA

Oh, were there? Why surely, one of
the sheets I needed to wrap up a
small present for Marcellina . . .

BARTOLO (*sarcastically*)

How nice of you! And the pen point . . .
Why is it wet from writing?

ROSINA (*aside*)

I could choke him!
(*aloud*) The pen point? I used it to
draw a flower for my needlework.

BARTOLO

Un fiore!

ROSINA

Un fiore.

BARTOLO

Un fiore!
Ah, fraschetta!

ROSINA

Davver.

BARTOLO

Zitta!

ROSINA

Credete.

BARTOLO

Basta così.

ROSINA

Signor . . .

BARTOLO

Non più . . . tacete.

A un dottor della mia sorte
queste scuse, signorina!
Vi consiglio, mia carina,
un po' meglio a imposturar.
I confetti alla ragazza!
Il ricamo sul tamburo!
Vi scottaste: eh via! eh via!
Ci vuol altro, figlia mia,
per potermi corbellar.
Perchè manca là quel foglio?
Vo' saper cotesto imbroglio.
Sono inutili le smorfie;
ferma là, non mi toccate!
Figlia mia, non lo sperate
ch'io mi lasci infinocchiar.
Via, carina, confessate;
son disposto a perdonar.
Non parlate? Vi ostinate?

So ben io quel che ho da far.
Signorina, un'altra volta
quandro Bartolo andrà fuori,
la consegna ai servitori
a suo modo far saprà.
Ah, non servono le smorfie,
faccia pur la gatta morta.
Cospetton! per quella porta
nemmen l'aria entrar potrà.
E Rosina innocentina,
sconsolata, disperata,
in sua camera serrata
fin ch'io voglio star dovrà.

(*Parte.*)

ROSINA

Brontola quanto vuoi,
chiudi porte e finestre. Io me ne
    rido:
già di noi femmine alla più marmotta
per aguzzar l'ingegno
e farla spiritosa tutto a un tratto
basta chiuderla a chiave e il colpo è
    fatto.

(*Parte*)

BERTA (*entrando*)

Finora in questa camera
mi parve di sentir un mormorio;
sarà stato il tutor; colla pupilla
non ha un'ora di ben . . . Queste ragazze
non la voglion capir.

(*Si batte alla porta.*)

Battono.

CONTE (*di dentro*)

Aprite.

BERTA

Vengo . . . Eccì . . . Ancora dura:
quel tabacco m'ha posto in sepoltura.

BARTOLO

A flower?

ROSINA

A flower!

BARTOLO

And I say that you didn't!

ROSINA

I did!

BARTOLO

Nonsense!

ROSINA

Believe me . . .

BARTOLO

You still deny it?

ROSINA

You're wrong.

BARTOLO

I'm right, be quiet!

To a man of my acumen
Do you offer lies and ruses?
I advise you in the future
To tell better lies by far.
Better, better, better, better!
It takes brighter girls to fool me,
My dear lady, than you are.
Brighter, brighter, brighter, brighter!
Do you think with lame excuses
Full of loopholes, ineffectual,
You can trick an intellectual,
Someone who's my mental par?
What a silly girl you are!
First you're wrapping up a present;
Then it's needlework and flowers;
Burned your finger, haha, what rot!
I advise you in the future
To invent a better plot.
Better, better, better, better!
Now I want to know the answer.
What has happened to that paper?
No more lying and protesting.
All your pouting will not help you.
Do you hear? You can't deceive me,
Never fear, no never, ever!
Yes, my lady, you are clever,
But I'm smarter than you are.
Say you're sorry, I'll forgive you.
I am willing to pardon you.
You are silent, you are mulish?
You won't answer? That is foolish.

Now I know what I will do,
How to punish girls like you.
Any time I have to leave you
I will give the servants orders
To be watching, to be watching
Ev'ry single breath you take.
Neither begging, crying, sighing,
Nor entreating, cheating, lying,
Will deter me or will sway me.
I will force you to obey me.
Like a shadow I will follow
Ev'ry single step you make.
And Rosina will be sitting
In her quarters, sewing, knitting;
And no begging, crying, sighing
Will deter me or will sway me.
No more flirting, no more flitting,
No more scheming and outwitting.
I will lock the doors and windows
Ev'ry minute, day and night.
I'll never let you out of sight.
My dear lady, all your ruses
Will not get you very far.
What a silly girl you are,
Ah, what a silly girl you are!
(*He leaves.*)

*ROSINA

Rant and rave forever; barricade the
doors and windows, I will defy you.
For any woman, be she ever so gentle,
will sharpen her wits, effectively op-
pose you and fight you. The more
you enslave her, the more she will
spite you. (*She leaves.*)

BERTHA (*enters*)

I thought I heard some arguing. The
doctor's angry voice, jabber, jabber,
jabber. That's my master for sure.
Rosina hates him. She's a stupid
young girl. Were I in her place, I
would know what to do.

(*A violent knocking is heard.*)
What's that again?

COUNT (*from outside*)

Do you hear me?

BERTHA

Coming. Kerchoo! Oh, what a madhouse!
In this place one has never one peaceful
moment.

———

This recitative is usually cut.

No. 11

Finale I

Il conte travestito da soldato di caval-
leria, indi Bartolo.

CONTE

Ehi, di casa!... buona gente!...
Ehi, di casa!...
niun risponde!

BARTOLO (*entrando*)

Chi è costui? che brutta faccia!
È ubbriaco! chi sarà?

CONTE

Ehi, di casa?...
maledetti!

BARTOLO

Cosa vuol, signor soldato?

CONTE

Ah!... sì,... sì,... bene-obbligato.
    (*Vedendolo, cerca in tasca.*)

BARTOLO

(Qui costui che mai vorrà?)

CONTE

Siete voi... Aspetta un poco...
Siete voi... dottor Balordo?

BARTOLO

Che Balordo?

CONTE (*leggendo*)

Ah, ah, Bertoldo?

BARTOLO

Che Bertoldo? Che Bertoldo?
Eh, andate al diavolo.
Dottor Bartolo.
Dottor Bartolo!

CONTE

Ah, bravissimo;
dottor barbaro;
benissimo.

BARTOLO

Un corno!

CONTE

Già v'è poca differenza!

BARTOLO

(Io già perdo la pazienza.

CONTE

(Non si vede! che impazienza!)

BARTOLO

(Qui prudenza ci vorrà.)

CONTE

Dunque voi... siete dottore?

BARTOLO

Son dottore, sì, signore.

CONTE

Va, benissimo; un abbraccio,
qua, collega.

BARTOLO

Indietro!

CONTE
(*lo abbraccia per forza*)

Qua. Sono anch'io dottor per cento,
maniscalco al reggimento.
    (*presentando il biglietto*)
Dell'alloggio sul biglietto
osservate, eccolo qua.

No. 11

Finale I

COUNT

(*He is disguised as a cavalry soldier and pretending to be drunk.*)

Hey, you people, do you hear me?
Where's the master? No one answers?
Hey?

BARTOLO (*entering*)

Who's the stranger? A drunken soldier?
I dislike him. Who is he?

COUNT

Hey, you people, what the devil!
Don't you hear me? Hey?

BARTOLO

What's your bus'ness, mister soldier?

COUNT

(*Noticing Bartolo, he searches for something in his pocket.*)

Ah! Let's see . . . I have the honor . . .

BARTOLO (*aside*)

What on earth does he want here?

COUNT

Am I talking . . . what does it say here . . .
To a certain . . . Doctor . . . Bolero?

BARTOLO (*furiously*)

What Bolero, what Bolero?

COUNT (*reading*)

I see . . . Bertoldo.

BARTOLO (*furiously*)

What Bertoldo, what Bertoldo?
I don't want intruders here.
Get the devil out of here!
My name is Bartolo,
Doctor Bartolo, Doctor Bartolo!

COUNT

Yes, I've got it now . . . Doctor Bungalow, sounds marvelous . . . Doctor Bungalow!

BARTOLO

Oh, hang it!

COUNT

I agree with you,
There's no diff'rence whatsoever.

BARTOLO (*aside*)

Now this bungler is beginning to annoy me.

COUNT (*aside*)

I don't see her, how annoying!
What in heaven does it mean?

BARTOLO (*aside*)

But I must not make a scene.

COUNT

So you say you are a doctor?

BARTOLO

Yes, I told you, I'm a doctor.

COUNT

That is excellent! We are colleagues.
Come, embrace me.

BARTOLO

Oh bother!

COUNT
(*insists on embracing him*)

There! We are colleagues by profession.
I'm the doctor for the horses.

(*presenting a paper*)

It is written on this paper . . .
Take a look and see for yourself.

(*aside*)

Ah, where is my dear beloved?
Where is she whom I adore?

BARTOLO

(Dalla rabbia, dal dispetto
io già crepo in verità.
Ah, ch'io fo, se mi ci metto,
qualche gran bestialità!)

(*Legge il biglietto.*)

CONTE

(Ah, venisse il caro oggetto
della mia felicità!
Vieni, vieni; il tuo diletto
pien d'amor t'attende già.)

ROSINA
(*Si arresta vedendo Bartolo.*)

Un soldato ed il tutore!
Cosa mai faranno qua?

(*Si avanza pian piano.*)

CONTE

(È Rosina; or son contento.)

ROSINA

(Ei mi guarda, s'avvicina.)

CONTE
(*piano a Rosina*)

(Son Lindoro.)

ROSINA

(Oh ciel! che sento!
Ah, giudizio, per pietà!)

BARTOLO (*vedendo Rosina*)

Signorina, che cercate?
Presto, presto, andate via.

ROSINA

Vado, vado, non gridate.

BARTOLO

Presto, presto, via di qua.

CONTE

Ehi, ragazza, vengo anch'io.

BARTOLO

Dove, dove, signor mio?

CONTE

In caserma, oh, questa è bella!

BARTOLO

In caserma? bagattella!

CONTE

Cara!

ROSINA

Aiuto!

BARTOLO

Olà, cospetto!

CONTE
(*a Bartolo incamminandosi verso
le camere*)

Dunque vado . . .

BARTOLO (*trattenendolo*)

Oh, no, signore,
qui d'alloggio non può star.

CONTE

Come? Come?

BARTOLO

Eh, non v'è replica:
ho il brevetto d'esenzione.

CONTE (*adirato*)

Il brevetto?

BARTOLO

Mio padrone,
un momento e il mostrerò.

(*Va allo scrittoio*)

BARTOLO (*aside*)

I am positively frantic,
I can't stand it any more!
One more insult, one more antic
And I'll throw him out the door.

COUNT

There is nothing more to fear, no,
And love will open ev'ry door.

ROSINA

(*enters, stops short on seeing a
stranger*)

There's my guardian, and a soldier
I have never seen before.
(*Rosina comes forward on tiptoe.*)

COUNT
(*seeing Rosina, to himself*)

It's Rosina, I am delighted.

ROSINA (*to herself*)

He is staring, coming nearer.

COUNT
(*softly to Rosina*)

I'm Lindoro.

ROSINA (*softly*)

My goodness gracious, careful, careful.
If he knows you, we are lost.

BARTOLO
(*noticing Rosina*)

Signorina, are we curious?
Kindly go about your bus'ness.

ROSINA

Always nasty, always furious.

BARTOLO

Hurry, hurry, hurry, hurry,
Hurry up, be on your way.

COUNT (*to Rosina*)

Wait a moment, I'll go with you.

BARTOLO

Just where do you think you're going?

COUNT

To my quarters, that's where I'm going!

BARTOLO

To your quarters? You are joking!

COUNT (*to Rosina*)

Darling . . .

ROSINA

Oh heavens!

BARTOLO (*to the Count*)

See here, you listen!

COUNT
(*to Bartolo, making his way toward
the inner rooms*)

Where's my room?

BARTOLO

You are mistaken,
You cannot stay in this house.

COUNT

And why can't I?

BARTOLO

Because I tell you so.

COUNT

You don't want me?

BARTOLO

It so happens I'm exempted.

COUNT (*angrily*)

You're exempted?

BARTOLO

I will show you in a moment,
It is here in black and white.
(*goes to the writingtable*)

CONTE

Ah, se qui restar non posso,
(*a Rosina*) (deh, prendete...)

ROSINA

(Ohimè, ci guarda!)

BARTOLO
(*cercando nello scrittoio*)

Ah, trovarlo ancor non posso.

ROSINA

(Prudenza!)

BARTOLO

Ma sì, sì, lo troverò.

CONTE

Cento smanie io sento addosso.
Ah, più reggere non so.

ROSINA

Cento smanie io sento addosso.
Ah, più reggere non so.

BARTOLO

Ah, ecco qua. (*legge*)
"*Con la presente il Dottor Bartolo
etcetera. Esentiamo...*"

CONTE
(*con un rovescio di mano manda
in aria la pergamena*)

Eh, andate al diavolo.
Non mi state più seccar.

BARTOLO

Cosa fa, signor mio caro?

CONTE

Zitto là, Dottor somaro.
Il mio alloggio è qui fissato,
e in alloggio qui vo' star.

BARTOLO

Vuol restar?

CONTE

Restar, sicuro,

BARTOLO (*prendendo un bastone*)

Oh, son stufo, mio padrone;
presto fuori, o un buon bastone
lo farà di qua sloggiar.

CONTE (*serio*)

Dunque lei... lei vuol battaglia?
Ben! Battaglia le vo' dar.
Bella cosa è una battaglia!
Ve la voglio qui mostrar.
(*avvicinandosi amichevolmente a
Bartolo*)
Osservate! questo è il fosso...
L'inimico voi sarete...

(*Gli dà una spinta.*)

Attenzione gli amici.

(*piano a Rosina alla quale si avvicina
porgendole la lettera*) (Giù il fazzoletto.)

E gli amici stan di qua.
Attenzion!

(*Lascia cadere il biglietto e Rosina vi fa
cadere sopra il fazzoletto.*)

BARTOLO

Ferma, ferma!

CONTE
(*rivolgendosi e fingendo accorgersi della
lettera che raccoglie*)

Che cos'è? ah!...

BARTOLO (*avvedendosene*)

Vo' vedere.

CONTE

Si, se fosse una ricetta!
Ma un biglietto... è mio dovere
Mi dovete perdonar.

(*Le dà il biglietto e il fazzoletto.*)

ROSINA

Grazie, grazie!

COUNT
(*softly to Rosina*)

While he's looking for his paper,
Take this letter.

ROSINA

Look out. He's watching.

BARTOLO
(*searching among his papers*)

Where the devil did I put it?

ROSINA
(*softly to the Count*)

Be careful.

BARTOLO

I am sure I have it here.

COUNT (*aside to Rosina*)

If he manages to find it,
We are lost; that much I know.

ROSINA AND COUNT

What an awkward situation,
How in heaven will it go?

BARTOLO

Ah! Here we are! (*reads: spoken*)
"Be it known herewith: Doctor Bartolo
    is exempted, etc."

COUNT
(*tossing the document into the
    air with his saber*)

Blast the silly document!
You are standing in my way.

BARTOLO

Have you gone completely crazy?

COUNT

In this house I have been quartered.
In this house I want to stay.

BARTOLO

In this house?

COUNT

Yes, I intend to.

BARTOLO (*furiously*)

Either you will go this minute,
Or a good old-fashioned beating
Will dispatch you on your way.
Get a move on, get a move on!

COUNT (*seriously*)

Oh, I see, you want a battle?
Fine! A battle it shall be.
I'm a soldier and like a battle.
Let us start it right away.
(*approaching Bartolo in a
    friendly way*)
This is my side, you're the enemy.
You're the foe . . . I am attacking,
(*thrusting at him*)
Now I'm storming the fortress.
(*aside to Rosina*)
Drop your handkerchief.
(*He drops a letter; Rosina lets her
    handkerchief fall upon it.*)
(*to Bartolo*)
You are fleeing. I have won.

BARTOLO
(*who has noticed the letter
    fall to the ground*)

Hold your forces!

COUNT

Surrender! Ah!

BARTOLO

Just a moment!

COUNT
(*pretending to catch sight of
    the letter, which he picks up*)

Wait, it might be a prescription.
No, just a letter, I must restore it
To the lady right away.
(*gives the letter and the
    handkerchief to Rosina*)

ROSINA

Thank you, thank you.

BARTOLO

Grazie un corno!
Qua quel foglio; impertinente!

(a Rosina)

A chi dico? Presto qua.

CONTE

Vuol battaglia?
Attenzion!

ROSINA

Ma quel foglio che chiedete,
per azzardo m'è cascato;
è la lista del bucato.

(Entrano da una parte Basilio con carte
in mano, dall'altra Berta.)

BARTOLO

Ah, fraschetta! Presto qua.

(Le strappa il foglio con violenza.)

Ah, che vedo! ho preso abbaglio!
È la lista, son di stucco!
Ah, son proprio un mammalucco!
Ah, che gran bestialità!

BERTA

Il barbiere...
Quanta gente!

ROSINA

Bravo, bravo
Il mammalucco
Che nel sacco
entrato è già.

BERTA

Non capisco, son di stucco;
Qualche imbroglio qui ci sta.

CONTE

Bravo, bravo,
Il mammalucco
Che nel sacco
entrato è già.

BARTOLO

Ah, son proprio un mammalucco!
Ah, che gran bestialità!

BASILIO

Sol, do, re, mi, fa,
re, sol, mi, la, fa, si, sol, do.
Ma che imbroglio è questo qua.

ROSINA

Ecco qua! Sempre un'istoria;
Sempre oppressa
e maltrattata;
Ah, che vita
disperata!
Non la so più sopportar.

BARTOLO (avvicindandosele)

Ah, Rosina...
Poverina...

CONTE

(minacciando e afferandolo per un
braccio)

Tu vien qua,
cosa l'hai fatto?

BARTOLO

Ah, fermate...
niente affato.

CONTE

(cavando la sciabola)

Ah, canaglia, traditore!

TUTTI (trattenendolo)

Via, fermatevi, signore.

CONTE

Io ti voglio subissar!

BARTOLO, BASILIO

Gente, aiuto, soccorrete mi!

ROSINA, BERTA

Gente, aiuto, ma chetatevi!

CONTE

Lasciatemi!

BARTOLO (*imitating Rosina*)

Thank you, thank you!
(*furiously*)
Let me have it, what's this paper?
Let me see it, I'm the master of this
house!

COUNT

You attack me? On your guard! Eeh!
ah!

ROSINA (*calmly*)

But of course I'll let you see it.
I was careless to have dropped it.
It's the list of last week's laundry.
(*gives Bartolo the laundry list
instead of the letter*)

BARTOLO
(*tearing the paper out of her hand*)

I'll believe it when I see it.
Let me read it; I must see it for myself.
(*reads*) "Seven night-shirts—"
I'm in a quand'ry.
She was right there; it's the laundry.

BERTHA (*re-enters*)

Still the soldier . . .
And my master . . .

BASILIO
(*enters, holding a music sheet*)

ROSINA

He's bewildered and befuddled,
He is in Lindoro's net;
He's bewildered and upset,
All befuddled and upset.

BERTHA

My poor brain is all befuddled,
How confusing things can get.

COUNT

I have caught him in my net,
He's bewildered and upset,
All befuddled and upset;
I have caught him in my net,
My clever net.

BARTOLO

I am muddled and befuddled,
I am totally upset.

BASILIO

(*sings from his music and conducts*)
Sol sol sol sol sol sol sol sol
Do re mi fa re sol mi,
La fa si sol do!
Ev'rybody is upset,
But the cause I don't know yet.

ROSINA (*in tears*)

That's too much! I cannot stand it,
Always scolded, always tortured and
tormented!
I am tired and disgusted,
I can't bear it any more!

BARTOLO (*approaching her*)

Poor Rosina, poor Rosina.

COUNT
(*threatening Bartolo*)

Awful man, what have you done now?

BARTOLO

You have done it, with your shouting.

COUNT
(*drawing his saber*)

Ah, you traitor, I will slay you!

ROSINA, BERTHA, BARTOLO, BASILIO

No more violence, I pray you!

COUNT

I will stab you through the heart!

ROSINA, BERTHA, BARTOLO, BASILIO

Someone help us quiet him!
Help, before it is too late!

COUNT

Let go of me, let go of me!

TUTTI

Gente, aiuto, per pietà.

Figaro entrando col bacile sotto il braccio, e detti.

FIGARO

Alto là!
Che cosa accadde,
signori miei?
Che chiasso è questo?
Eterni Dei!
Già sulla strada
a questo strepito
s'è radunata
mezza città.

(*piano al Conte*)

Signor, giudizio,
per carità.

BARTOLO (*additando il Conte*)

Quest'è un birbante...

CONTE (*additando Bartolo*)

Quest'è un briccone...

BARTOLO

Ah, disgraziato!

CONTE (*minacciando colla sciabola*)

Ah, maledetto!

FIGARO
(*alzando il bacile e minacciando
il Conte*)

Signor soldato, porti rispetto,
o questo fusto, corpo del diavolo,
or la creanza le insegnerà.
(Signor, giudizio, per carità.)

CONTE (*a Bartolo*)

Brutto scimmiotto!

BARTOLO (*al Conte*)

Birbo malnato!

TUTTI (*a Bartolo*)

Zitto, dottore...

BARTOLO

Voglio gridare...

TUTTI (*al Conte*)

Fermo, signore...

CONTE

Voglio ammazzare...

TUTTI

Fate silenzio,
per carità.

CONTE

No, voglio ucciderlo,
non v'è pietà.

(*Si ode bussare con violenza alla porta
di strada.*)

TUTTI

Zitti, ché bussano.
Che mai sarà?

BARTOLO

Chi è?

UN UFFICIALE (*di dentro*)

La forza!

CORO (*di dentro*)

La forza,
aprite qua.

TUTTI

La forza!
Oh diavolo!

FIGARO E BASILIO

L'avete fatta!

CONTE E BARTOLO

Niente paura. Venga pur qua.

FIGARO
(enters with a shaving basin)

Stop and wait!
Why this confusion, would you mind
  telling?
What is this bedlam, screaming and
  yelling?
Out on the plaza people are gathering.
You are arousing half of the town.
        (aside to the Count)
Sir, I entreat you, please quiet down!

BARTOLO
(pointing to the Count)

He is the culprit!

COUNT *(pointing to Bartolo)*

He is a tyrant!

BARTOLO *(to the Count)*

You are a bandit!

COUNT
*(threatening Bartolo with his
  drawn saber)*

You are a bully!

FIGARO
*(raising his basin as if he were
  threatening the Count)*

Dear mister soldier, it is essential
You be respectful, more deferential,
Or on my honor, I'll take my razor-
  strap
And teach you manners once and for
  all.
        (aside to the Count)
Sir, I entreat you, not quite so rough.

COUNT *(to Bartolo)*

Ugly gorilla!

BARTOLO *(to the Count)*

You are a monster!

ROSINA, BERTHA, FIGARO, BASILIO

Doctor, be quiet!

BARTOLO

I feel like yelling!

ROSINA, BERTHA, FIGARO, BASILIO

You, too, be quiet!

COUNT

I feel like killing!

ROSINA, BERTHA, FIGARO, BASILIO

Better not try it.
That is enough.

COUNT

No, I must murder him! Yes, he must
  die!

ROSINO, BERTHA, FIGARO, BASILIO

Better not try it.
Let it go by!
        (A loud knocking is heard.)

ROSINA, BERTHA, FIGARO
(thunderstruck)

What does that knocking mean?

ALL

What can it be?

BARTOLO *(spoken)*

Who's there?

OFFICER OF THE GUARD
(from outside)

Police!

THE GUARD *(from outside)*

Police force, police force.
Unlock the door, unlock the door!

ALL *(on stage)*

We're done for!
The law is here!

FIGARO, BASILIO

We are in trouble, What shall we do
  now?

COUNT, BARTOLO

Do not be frightened, let them come in.

TUTTI

Quest'avventura,
ah, come diavolo mai finirà!

CORO

Fermi tutti.
Nessun si mova.
Miei signori, che si fa?
Questo chiasso donde è nato?
La cagione presto qua.

BARTOLO

Questa bestia di soldato,
mio signor, m'ha maltrattato.
Sì, signor, sì, signor,
m'ha maltratto.

FIGARO

Io qua venni, mio signore,
questo chiasso ad acquetare.
Sì, signor, sì, signor,
questo chiasso ad acquetare.

BASILIO

Fa un inferno di rumore,
parla sempre d'ammazzare.
Sì, signor, sì, signor,
parla sempre d'ammazzare.

CONTE

In alloggio quel briccone
non mi volle qui accettare.
Sì, signor, sì, signor,
non mi volle qui accettare.

ROSINA

Perdonate, poverino,
tutto effetto fu del vino.
Sì, signor, sì, signor.

BERTA

Fa un interno di rumore
parla sempre d'ammazzare.
Sì, signor, sì, signor.

UFFICIALE

Ho inteso. (al Conte)
Galantuom, siete in arresto.
Fuori presto, via di qua.

(I soldati muovono per circondare il
   Conte)

CONTE

Io in arresto?
Fermi, olà.

(Con gesto autorevole trattiene i soldati
che si arrestano. Egli chiama a se
l'Ufficiale, gli dà a leggere un foglio:
l'Ufficiale resta sopreso, vuol fargli
un inchino, e il Conte lo tratienne.
l'Ufficiale fa cenno ai soldati che si
ritirano indietro, e anch'egli fa lo
stesso. Quadro di stupore.)

ROSINA

Fredda ed immobile
come una statua

ROSINA E BERTA

fiato non restami
da respirar.

CONTE

Freddo ed immobile
come una statua,
fiato non restagli
da respirar.

BARTOLO

Freddo ed immobile
come una statua
fiato non restami
da respirar.

BASILIO

Freddo ed immobile
fiato non restami
da respirar.

FIGARO

Guarda Don Bartolo!
Sembra una statua!
Ah, ah! dal ridere
sto per crepar.

ROSINA, BERTHA

We are in trouble. What shall we do
now?

(*The guard enters.*)

ALL

How to get out of this, how to begin?

THE GUARD (*enters*)

Pay attention and answer clearly.
Say what happened, here and now.
Who has started this commotion?
Who began this awful row?
Who is guilty, and why, and where and
how?

BARTOLO

This barbarian of a soldier
Nearly killed me with his saber.
Yes he did, yes he did,
Nearly killed me with his saber.

FIGARO

I came here to keep them quiet,
That is all I tried to do.
Yes I did, yes I did.
That is all I tried to do.

BASILIO

He was acting like a madman,
Always brandishing his saber.
Yes he did, yes he did.
It is absolutely true.

COUNT

I am quartered with the doctor,
And he made a big to-do.
Yes he did, yes he did.
Yes, he made a big to-do.

ROSINA

You can see that he's been drinking
And is hazy in his thinking.
Yes he is, yes he is.

BERTHA

He was acting like a madman,
Always brandishing his saber.
Yes he did, yes he did.

OFFICER

So that's it.
(*to the Count*)
So it's you. I must arrest you,
Off to prison, come at once.

(*The soldiers advance
to surround the Count.*)

COUNT

You arrest me, really?
Not a chance!

(*He takes the officer aside and shows
him a paper. The officer is astonished, orders the guard to retire to
the back, where he places himself at
their head. All stand rigid in amaze-
ment.*)

ROSINA AND BERTHA

(*as if spellbound*)

Rigid and motionless,
Like a marble monument,
I cannot stir a step,
I can't draw a breath.

COUNT

Rigid and motionless,
Like a marble monument,
They cannot stir a step,
They can't draw a breath.

BARTOLO (*as if spellbound*)

Rigid and motionless,
Like a marble monument,
I cannot stir a step,
I can't draw a breath.

BASILIO (*as if spellbound*)

Rigid and motionless,
I cannot stir a step,
I can't draw a breath.

FIGARO

Look at Don Bartolo,
Rigid and motionless,
Just like a monument.
Ha, ha, I laugh myself
Almost to death.

BARTOLO

(all Ufficiale)

Ma, signor . . .

CORO

Zitto tu!

BARTOLO

Ma un dottor . . .

CORO

Oh non più!

BARTOLO

Ma se lei? . . .

CORO

Non parlar . . .

BARTOLO

Ma vorrei . . .

CORO

Non gridar.

BARTOLO, BASILIO

Ma se noi . . .

CORO

Zitti voi.

ROSINA, BARTOLO, BASILIO

Ma se poi.

CORO

Pensiam noi.

ROSINA, BARTOLO, BASILIO

Ma se noi.

CORO

Non parlar.
Vada ognun pci fatti suoi,
si finisca d'altercar.

BARTOLO

Ma sentite . . .

COUNT, FIGARO

Zitto su!

ROSINA, BERTA, BASILIO

Zitto giù!

BARTOLO

Ma ascoltate . . .

COUNT, FIGARO

Zitto qua!

ROSINA, BERTA, BASILIO

Zitto là!

BARTOLO

Ma sentite!
Ascoltate!

TUTTI

Mi par d'essere con la testa
in un'orrida fucina,
dove cresce e mai non resta
delle incudini sonore
l'importuno strepitar.
Alternando questo e quello
pesantissimo martello
fa con barbara armonia
muri e vôlte rimbombar.
E il cervello, poverello,
già stordito, sbalordito,
non ragiona, si confonde,
si riduce ad impazzar.

BARTOLO
(*suddenly breaking the spell*)

But I don't . . .

GUARD

Hold your tongue!

BARTOLO

No, I won't . . .

GUARD

You are wrong.

BARTOLO

I protest . . .

GUARD

What about?

BARTOLO

I request . . .

GUARD

Do not shout!

BARTOLO AND BASILIO

Then I will . . .

GUARD

You'll be still!

ROSINA, BARTOLO, BASILIO

But suppose . . .

GUARD

No one knows.

ROSINA, BARTOLO, BASILIO

But if you . . .

GUARD

That will do.

ROSINA, BARTOLO, BASILIO

You are wrong . . .

GUARD

We are right.
Each one go about his bus'ness.
We have come to end the fight.

COUNT, FIGARO

That will do.

ROSINA, BERTHA, BASILIO

That will do!

COUNT, FIGARO

That is true!

ROSINA, BARTHA, BASILIO

That is true!

COUNT, FIGARO

End the fight.

ROSINA, BERTHA, BASILIO

End the fight!

COUNT, FIGARO

You are right.

ROSINA, BERTHA, BASILIO

You are right!

BARTOLO

But I tell you, you must listen . . .

ALL SOLOISTS
(*except the officer*)

My poor head is madly reeling,
Like a mighty millstone wheeling.
Like a heavy hammer sounding,
On the anvil loudly pounding,
Rolling, crashing, never resting,
Like a millstone grinding, turning,
Winding, churning,
Till my throbbing brain is numb.
Like a hammer rising, falling,
With a din that is appalling,
So barbaric, so infernal
That the very walls succumb.

BARTOLO

Alternando
questo quello,

BASILIO

Alternando
questo quello,

CORO

Alternando questo quello,

TUTTI

E il cervello, poverello,
già stordito, sbalordito,
non ragiona, si confonde,
si riduce ad impazzar.

FINE DELL'ATTO PRIMO

ATTO SECONDO
SCENA PRIMA

Camera ad uso di studio in casa di Bar-
tolo con sedia ed un pianoforte con
varie carte di musica.

No. 12

Recitativo e Duetto

BARTOLO

Ma vedi il mio destino! Quel soldato,
per quanto abbia cercato,
niun lo conosce in tutto il reggimento.
Io dubito . . . eh, cospetto!
Che dubitar? Scommetto
che dal conte Almaviva
è stato qui spedito quel signore
ad esplorar della Rosina il core.
Nemmeno in casa propria
sicuri si può star! Ma io . . .

(Battono.)

Chi batte?
Ehi, chi è di là . . . Battono, non
    sentite?
In casa io son; non v'è timore, aprite.

CONTE

(travestito da maestro di musica)

Pace e gioia sia con voi.

BARTOLO

Mille grazie, non s'incomodi.

CONTE

Gioia e pace per mill'anni.

BARTOLO

Obbligato in verità.

CONTE

Pace e gioia sia con voi.

BARTOLO

Mille grazie, non s'incomodi.
(Questo volto non m'è ignoto)

CONTE

(Ah, se un colpo è andato
    a vuoto . . .)

BARTOLO

(non ravviso, non ricordo)

CONTE

(a gabbar questo balordo)

BARTOLO

(ma quel volto, ma quell'abito)

CONTE

(un novel travestimento)

BARTOLO

(non capisco . . . chi sarà?)

CONTE

(più propizio a me sarà.)
Gioia e pace, pace e gioia!

BARTOLO

Ho capito. (Oh! ciel! che noia!)

BARTOLO

Now it's rising.

BASILIO

Now it's falling.

GUARD

Now it's rising, now it's falling.

ALL

And the swelling, and the yelling
Will not finish or diminish.
Never ceasing, but increasing
Till it makes me deaf and dumb,
Till at last my throbbing brain is
dazed and numb.

End of Act I

ACT TWO

Scene I

*The music room of Doctor Bartolo.
There is some music on the piano.*

No. 12

Recitative and Duettino

BARTOLO (*alone*)

It's just as I suspected; all my efforts
to learn that soldier's name proved to
be futile. It seems that no one knows
him. I'm wondering . . . oh, I've
got it! It's clear as day! I'll wager
that this drunkard of a soldier is no
one but a scout of Almaviva's. One
of his spies, trying to see Rosina.
Even in one's own house one is no
longer safe. From now on . . .
(*knocking is heard*) Who's knocking? Who can it be? Ambrosius, go
and open. Don't be afraid. If it's
Basilio, admit him.

COUNT

(*enters disguised as a music master,
in a robe and hat similar to Don
Basilio's*)
(*with an oily voice*)

Heaven bless you, now and ever.

BARTOLO

Thank you, thank you, for your com-
pliment.

COUNT

Heaven bless you ever after.

BARTOLO

I am honored, you're very kind.

COUNT

Heaven bless you, now and ever.

BARTOLO

Thank you, thank you, for your senti-
ment.
(*to himself*)
I have seen that fellow somewhere.

COUNT (*to himself*)

I have not achieved my purpose . . .

BARTOLO (*to himself*)

He looks awfully familiar.

COUNT

In the morning as a soldier . . .

BARTOLO (*to himself*)

Who the devil is this creature?

COUNT (*to himself*)

But disguised as a music teacher . . .

BARTOLO (*to himself*)

Will my trouble never end?

COUNT (*to himself*)

I am sure to reach my end,
Yes, I will reach my end.
(*aloud*)
Heaven bless you now and ever.

BARTOLO

(*becoming impatient*)

I have heard you, how repetitious.

CONTE

Gioia e pace, ben di core.

BARTOLO

Basta, basta, per pietà.

CONTE

Gioia.

BARTOLO

Gioia.

CONTE

Pace.

BARTOLO

Pace.
(Ma che perfido destino!
Ma che barbara giornata!
Tutti quanti a me davanti!
Che crudel fatalità!)

CONTE

(Il vecchion non mi conosce:
oh, mia sorte fortunata!
Ah, mio ben! Fra pochi istanti
parlerem con libertà.)

BARTOLO

Insomma, mio signore,
chi è lei, si può sapere?

CONTE

Don Alonso,
professore di musica ed allievo
di Don Basilio.

BARTOLO

Ebbene?

CONTE

Don Basilio
sta male, il poverino, ed in sua vece . . .

BARTOLO (*in atto di partire*)

Sta mal? Corro a verderlo.

CONTE (*trattenendolo*)

Piano, piano.
Non è mal così grave.

BARTOLO

(Di costui non mi fido.) (*risoluto*)
Andiamo, andiamo.
                    (*risoluto*)

CONTE

Ma signore . . .

BARTOLO (*brusco*)
Che c'è?

CONTE (*tirandolo a parte*)

Voleva dirvi . . .

BARTOLO
Parlate forte.

CONTE (*sottovoce*)
Ma . . .

BARTOLO (*sdegnato*)

Forte, vi dico.

COUNT

Heaven bless you ever after.

BARTOLO

So you told me, my good friend.

COUNT

Heaven . . .

BARTOLO
(*imitating*)

Heaven . . .

COUNT

Bless you . . .

BARTOLO (*imitating*)

Bless you.
I have heard you, no more good
  wishes.

COUNT

Heaven bless you ever after.

BARTOLO
(*imitating*)

Ever after —
Stop it, stop it, let me be.
          (*to himself*)
What a terrible disaster!

COUNT (*to himself*)

As a humble music master . . .

BARTOLO (*to himself*)

What a day of toil and trouble.

COUNT (*to himself*)

I will certainly deceive him.

BARTOLO (*to himself*)

Ev'rybody is conspiring,
Ev'ryone is after me.

COUNT (*to himself*)

Ah, my darling, the time is nearing
When at last you will be free.

BARTOLO

And now, if I may ask, who are
  you? Why did you come here?

COUNT
(*disguising his voice*)

Don Alonso, a professor of music and
  pupil of Don Basilio.

BARTOLO

And your bus'ness?

COUNT
(*disguising his voice*)

Don Basilio, my dear beloved master,
  is indisposed.

BARTOLO (*concerned*)

He's ill? I'll go and see him.
(*He is about to leave.*)

COUNT (*detaining him*)

Just a moment, it is not quite so
  serious.

BARTOLO (*aside*)

This man is a swindler. (*resolved, to
  the Count*) You heard me, I'm going.

COUNT

Not so hasty.

BARTOLO (*roughly*)

Why not?

COUNT (*in a low voice*)

You haven't heard yet . . .

BARTOLO

Can't you speak louder?

COUNT (*in a whisper*)

But . . .

BARTOLO (*angrily*)

Louder, I tell you!

CONTE (*sdegnato anch'esso e alzando la voce*)

Ebbene, come volete,
ma chi sia Don Alonso apprenderete.

    (*in atto di partire*)

Vo dal conte Almaviva . . .

BARTOLO
(*trattenendolo con dolcezza*)

Piano, piano.
Dite, dite, v'ascolto.

CONTE (*a voce alta e sdegnata*)

Il conte . . .

BARTOLO

Piano.
per carità.

CONTE (*calmandosi*)

Stamane
nella stessa locanda
era meco d'alloggio, ed in mie mani
per caso capitò questo biglietto

    (*mostrando un biglietto*)

dalla vostra pupilla a lui diretto.

BARTOLO
(*prendendo il biglietto e guardandolo*)

Che vedo! è sua scrittura!

CONTE

Don Basilio
nulla sa di quel foglio: ed io, per lui
venendo a dar lezione alla ragazza,
voleva farmene un merito con voi . . .
perchè . . . con quel biglietto . . .

    (*mendicando un ripiego con qualche imbarazzo*)

si potrebbe . . .

BARTOLO

Che cosa?

CONTE

Vi dirò . . .
s'io potessi parlare alla ragazza,
io creder . . . verbigrazia . . . le farei
che me lo diè del Conte un'altra amante,
prova significante
che il Conte di Rosina si fa gioco.
E perciò . . .

BARTOLO

Piano un poco.
Una calunnia! Oh bravo!
Degno e vero scolar di Don Basilio!

(*Lo abbraccia, e mette in tasca il biglietto.*)

Io saprò come merita
ricompensar sì bel suggerimento.
Vo a chiamar la ragazza;
poichè tanto per me v'interessate,
mi raccomando a voi.

CONTE

Non dubitate.

(*Bartolo entra nella camera di Rosina.*)

L'affare del biglietto
dalla bocca m'è uscito non volendo.
Ma come far? Senza un tal ripiego
mi toccava andar via come un baggiano.
Il mio disegno a lei
ora paleserò; s'ella acconsente,
io son felice appieno.
Eccola. Ah, il cor sento balzarmi in seno!

BARTOLO

Venite, signorina. Don Alonso,
che qui vedete, or vi darà lezione.

ROSINA (*vedendo il Conte*)

Ah! . . .

BARTOLO

Cos'è stato?

ROSINA

È un granchio al piede.

CONTE

Oh nulla!
sedete a me vicin, bella fanciulla.
Se non vi spiace, un poco di lezione,
di Don Basilio invece, vi darò.

ROSINA

Oh, con mio gran piacer la prenderò.

COUNT
(*angry, in a very loud voice*)

All right, if you insist; but you might not be happy at what I'll tell you.
(*louder*)
It's about Count Almaviva . . .

BARTOLO (*alarmed*)

Softer, softer, I am not hard of hearing.

COUNT (*loudly and angrily*)

The Count . . .

BARTOLO

Ssh! For goodness' sake.

COUNT (*lowering his voice*)

All right, then. It so happens I'm lodging at the inn where the Count stays, and by some chance I came into possession of this little letter (*showing him a letter*) which Rosina has sent him. See for yourself.

BARTOLO
(*taking the letter and looking at it*)

Rosina. It is her writing.

COUNT

Don Basilio does not know that I have it, and since I came to give the girl her lesson in his place, I am most anxious to merit your approval because (*seeking an excuse*) this little message could be useful.

BARTOLO

For what?

COUNT

I'll explain: if I could for a moment talk to Rosina, I'd tell her that I saw it in the hands — uh — of a certain lady who is his mistress; thus rousing a suspicion that the Count betrays Rosina with a mistress. In that case . . .

BARTOLO

Just a moment. That would be slander. How clever! I see that you went to school with Don Basilio. (*embraces him and puts the letter in his pocket*) You are right. I appreciate what you have done and you will find me grateful. You may talk to Rosina. I will call her at once. You're very helpful, you are a friend in need.

COUNT (*ambiguously*)

Oh yes, indeed!
(*Bartolo enters an inner room. To himself, with his natural voice*)
The story is fantastic, but I had to say something to convince him. What could I do? If I had not done it, he'd have chased me away like any beggar. But now that I shall see her, ev'rything will go well. If she accepts me, my joy would know no measure. There she is! My heart beats with delight and pleasure.

BARTOLO
(*enters, leading Rosina*)

Come, come, my dear Rosina, don't be bashful. Meet Don Alonso. Today he'll give you your lesson.

ROSINA
(*seeing the Count*)

Ah!

BARTOLO

What's the matter?

ROSINA
(*pretending to have hurt her foot*)

I have sprained my ankle.

COUNT

I'm sorry! Sit down here by the piano for a while. I have the pleasure, in place of Don Basilio, to give you your lesson for today.

ROSINA

It makes me very happy that you have come.

CONTE

Che volete cantar?

ROSINA

Io canto, se le aggrada,
il rondò dell'INUTIL PRECAU-
ZIONE.

BARTOLO

Eh sempre, sempre in bocca
l'INUTIL PRECAUZIONE!

ROSINA

Io ve l'ho detto:
è il titolo dell'opera novella.

BARTOLO

Or bene, intesi; andiamo.

ROSINA

Eccolo qua.

CONTE

Da brava, incominciamo.

(Il Conte siede al pianoforte e Rosina
canta accompagnata dal Conte; Bartolo siede ed ascolta.)

No. 13

Duetto

ROSINA

Contro un cor che accende amore
di verace invitto ardore,
s'arma invan poter tiranno
di rigor, di crudeltà.
D'ogni assalto vincitore
sempre amore trionferà.
Ah Lindoro, mio tesoro,
se sapessi, se vedessi!
Questo cane di tutore,
ah, che rabbia che mi fa!
Caro, a te mi raccomando,
tu mi salva, per pietà.

CONTE

Non temer, ti rassicura;
sorte amica a noi sarà.

ROSINA

Dunque spero?

CONTE

A me t'affida.

ROSINA

E il mio cor?

CONTE

Giubilerà.

ROSINA

Cara immagine ridente,
dolce idea d'un lieto amore,
tu m'accendi in petto il core,
tu mi porti a delirar.

No. 14

Recitativo ed Arietta

CONTE

Bella voce! Bravissima!

ROSINA

Oh! mille grazie!

BARTOLO

Certo, bella voce,
ma quest'aria, cospetto! è assai noiosa;
la musica a' miei tempi era altra cosa.
Ah! quando per esempio
cantava Caffariello
quell'aria portentosa la, ra, la...
sentite, Don Alonso: eccola qua.
Quando mi sei vicina,
amabile Rosina...
l'aria dicea Giannina,
ma io dico Rosina...

COUNT

And what will you sing?

ROSINA

I'll sing with your permission, an air from *The Superfluous Precaution.*

BARTOLO

That's all she ever thinks of: *The Superfluous Precaution.*

ROSINA

As I have told you, it's an opera and popular this season.

BARTOLO

Yes, yes, dear, I know. Let's hear it.

ROSINA

Here is the score.

COUNT

(*seats himself at the piano; Bartolo takes a seat and listens.*)

No. 13

Duet

*ROSINA

(*sings to the Count's accompaniment*)

There's no force, no might or power
Strong enough to destroy a love in
    flower.
No assault by heartless tyrants
Makes it fail or fade or fall.
Holding firmer than a tower,
Love will triumph and conquer all.
Ah, Lindoro, dear Lindoro,
If you knew what I must suffer!
My intolerable tutor
Very soon will drive me mad.
You must help me, you must save me,
Or my fate will be too bad.

————

This aria is usually replaced by another coloratura aria, suited to the period of the opera.

COUNT

Trust in me, and I assure you,
I will free you, Rosina dear.

ROSINA

Will you really?

COUNT

You have my promise.

ROSINA

And our love?

COUNT

Will never fail.

ROSINA

How your words console and cheer me
With the new hope that they impart.
There is no one I love more dearly,
You alone have won my heart.

No. 14

Recitative and Arietta

COUNT

What an artist! Bravissimo!

ROSINA

You're very gracious.

BARTOLO

Surely, she's an artist. But that dissonant music! I cannot stand it. In my day, it was diff'rent. Then we had tunes. For instance that great tenor, Ca-ca-ca-Caffariello, he sang that minuetto . . . dadadadada . . . Now that's what I call music! There, play for me.

(*The Count accompanies him, while he sings.*)

All of the world looks greener,
When I am near Rosina . . .

(*He interrupts his song.*)

Actually it's "Giannina" but I changed it to "Rosina."

(*Entra Figaro col bacile sotto il braccio,
e si pone dietro Bartolo imitando
il canto con caricatura.*)

Il cor mi brilla in petto,
mi balla il minuetto . . .

BARTOLO (*avvedendosi di Figaro*)

Bravo, signor barbiere,
ma bravo!

FIGARO

Eh, niente affatto:
scusi, son debolezze.

BARTOLO

Ebben, guidone,
che vieni a fare?

FIGARO

Oh bella!
Vengo a farvi la barba: oggi vi tocca.

BARTOLO

Oggi non voglio.

FIGARO

Oggi non vuol? Domani
non potrò io.

BARTOLO

Perchè?

FIGARO

(*Lascia sul tavolo il bacile e cava un
libro di memorie.*)

Perchè ho da fare
a tutti gli ufficiali
del nuovo reggimento barba e testa . . .
alla marchesa Andronica
il biondo parrucchin coi maronè . . .
al contino Bombè
il ciuffo a campanile . . .
purgante all'avvocato Bernardone
che ieri s'ammalò d'indigestione . . .
e poi . . . e poi . . . che serve?
(*riponendosi in tasca il libro*)
Doman non posso.

BARTOLO

Orsù, meno parole.
Oggi non vo' far barba.

FIGARO

No? Cospetto!
Guardate che avventori!
Vengo stamane: in casa v'è l'inferno;
ritorno dopo pranzo: oggi non vog-
lio.
(*contraffacendolo*)
Ma che? M'avete preso
per un qualche barbier da contadini?
Chiamate pur un altro, io me ne vado.
(*Riprende il bacile in atto di partire.*)

BARTOLO

Che serve? . . . a modo suo;
vedi che fantasia!
Va in camera a pigliar la biancheria.
(*Si cava dalla cintola un mazzo di
chiavi per darle a Figaro, indi le
ritira.*)
No, vado io stesso.
(*Entra.*)

FIGARO

(Ah, se mi dava in mano
il mazzo delle chiavi, ero a cavallo.)
(*a Rosina*)
Dite: non è fra quelle
la chiave che apre quella gelosia?

ROSINA

Sì, certo; è la più nuova.

BARTOLO (*rientrando*)

(Ah, son pur buono
a lasciar qua quel diavol di barbiere!)
Animo, va tu stesso.
(*dando le chiavi a Figaro*)
Passato il corridor, sopra l'armadio
il tutto troverai.
Bada, non toccar nulla.

FIGARO

Eh, non son matto.
(Allegri!) Vado e torno. (Il colpo è
fatto.)
(*Entra.*)
BARTOLO (*al Conte*)
È quel briccon, che al **Conte**
ha portato il biglietto di **Rosina**.

(*He continues, illustrating the song with dancing motions. Figaro enters, with his basin and razor. He stands still behind Bartolo and imitates him.*)

All of the world looks greener,
When I am near Rosina.
My heart is gay and sprightly,
My feet are dancing lightly.

(*He dances.*)

BARTOLO (*noticing Figaro*)

That's not very funny, mister barber!

FIGARO

Please do not mind me; really, I could not help it.

BARTOLO

All right, you prankster, why did you come here?

FIGARO

Now hear that! I want to give you your shave. This is your day.

BARTOLO

Today I cannot.

FIGARO

Today you cannot? Tomorrow, to-morrow *I* can't.

BARTOLO

Why not?

FIGARO

Because I'm busy. (*puts his basin on a table, and takes a notebook out of his pocket*)
I'm shaving all the officers of the regiment in town, even the colonel; the Countess Andronica has called me to her house to do her hair; the Viscount of Bombé must have a wig with ringlets; and then I have to tend to Don Pasquale — last night he had a fit of indigestion — and then some errands. (*He puts the book in his pockets*) Oh, well, tomorrow I'm busy.

BARTOLO

All right, don't talk so much; today there'll be no shaving.

FIGARO

So? No shaving? Is ev'rybody crazy? I call in the morning, the whole place is a madhouse. I try it after dinner: (*imitating Bartolo*) "today, no shaving." Look here; am I your barber or one of your dumb, half-witted servants? I can no longer stand it. (*taking his basin as though about to go*) No, sir, I am quitting.

BARTOLO

It's no use. I'm at his mercy, he acts like a prima donna. Then quickly go to my room, and get a towel. (*He takes a bunch of keys from his belt and gives them to Figaro, but then takes them back again.*) No, I'll go myself.

FIGARO (*aside*)

Ah, if somehow I could manage to borrow his whole key ring, that would be perfect. (*to Rosina*) Tell me, on his key ring, which key is the one that fits the balcony?

ROSINA

The new one; it's also the biggest.

BARTOLO (*returning*)

No, I was stupid. I can't leave them alone here with the barber. Figaro, take my key ring and go into my room. (*giving the keys to Figaro*) There on the washstand, you'll find all that is needed. Careful, don't touch my china.

FIGARO

Oh, don't worry. (*to himself*) An idea! (*aloud*) Yes, sir, the china. (*aside*) It could not be finer. (*He goes into Bartolo's room.*)

BARTOLO

(*to the Count, confidentially*)

That is the rogue who this morning took Rosina's letter to the Count.

CONTE

Mi sembra un imbroglion di prima
  sfera.

BARTOLO

Eh, a me non me la ficca . . .

(*Si sente di dentro un gran rumor
  come di vasellame che si spezza.*)

Ah, disgraziato me!

ROSINA

Ah, che rumore!

BARTOLO

Oh, che briccon! Me lo diceva il core.

(*Entra.*)

CONTE (*a Rosina*)

Quel Figaro è un grand'uomo; or che
  siam soli,
ditemi, o cara: il vostro al mio destino
d'unir siete contenta?
Franchezza!

ROSINA (*con entusiasmo*)

Ah, mio Lindoro,
altro io non bramo . . .

(*Si ricompone vedendo rientrar Bartolo
  e Figaro.*)

CONTE

Ebben?

BARTOLO

Tutto m'ha rotto;
sei piatti, otto bicchieri, una terrina.

FIGARO

(*mostrando di soppiatto al Conte la
  chiave della gelosia che avrà rubata
  dal mazzo*)

Vedete che gran cosa! Ad una chiave
se io non m'attaccava per fortuna,
per quel maledettissimo
corridor così oscuro,
spezzato mi sarei la testa al muro.
Tiene ogni stanza al buio, e poi . . .
  e poi . . .

BARTOLO

Oh, non più.

FIGARO

Dunque andiam.
(*al Conte e Rosina*)
Giudizio.

BARTOLO

A noi.
(*Si dispone per sedere a farsi radere.
  In quella entra Basilio.*)

No. 15

Scena e Quintetto

ROSINA

(Don Basilio!)

CONTE

(Cosa veggo!)

FIGARO

(Quale intoppo!)

BARTOLO

Come qua?

BASILIO

Servitor di tutti quanti.

BARTOLO

(Che vuol dir tal novità?)

CONTE *e* FIGARO

(Qui franchezza ci vorrà.)

ROSINA

(Ah, di noi che mai sarà?)

BARTOLO

Don Basilio, come state?

BASILIO (*stupito*)

Come sto?

COUNT

He seems to be a very crafty fellow.

BARTOLO

Yes, he is, but I am craftier.
(*A great crash of china and glass break-
ing is heard.*)
Ah, what has happened now?

ROSINA

What was that noise?

BARTOLO

That clumsy oaf! I had a premonition!
(*He goes to see what happened.*)

COUNT (*to Rosina*)

Our Figaro is priceless! Now, my beloved, answer me, my darling. Are
you willing to be my wife, to share
your life with me? Speak frankly.

ROSINA (*ardently*)

Ah, my Lindoro, there's nothing I wish
more.
(*Bartolo and Figaro re-enter.*)

COUNT

What was it?

BARTOLO

Ev'rything's in shambles. My china, my
precious glasses in a thousand pieces!

FIGARO

It could have been much worse, (*sec-
retly showing to the Count the key
of the balcony which he has taken
off the bunch*) but I was lucky and
stumbled on a key I could hold
on to. I could not see my hand in
front of my face in the darkness. I
almost broke my neck when I slip-
ped. Why can't they leave a light
on? Moreover, moreover . . .

BARTOLO

All right, all right.

FIGARO

Can we start?
(*to the Count and Rosina*)
Be careful.

BARTOLO

I'm ready. (*settles himself in a chair
to be shaved. Don Basilio enters un-
expectedly.*)

No. 15

Quintet

ROSINA

Don Basilio!

COUNT

Heaven help us!

FIGARO

That means trouble.

BARTOLO

How is this?

BASILIO (*ceremoniously*)

It is I, your devoted, humble servant.

BARTOLO

This is really a surprise.

ROSINA (*to herself*)
Dare I believe my eyes?

COUNT (*softly to Figaro*)
Now it's time to improvise . . .

FIGARO (*softly to the Count*)
And invent some clever lies.

BARTOLO
(*getting up from his chair*)
Don Basilio, do you feel better?

BASILIO (*astonished*)
Better, how?

FIGARO (*interrompendo*)

Or che s'aspetta?
Questa barba benedetta
la facciamo sì o no?

BARTOLO (*a Figaro*)

Ora vengo!
(*a Basilio*)
E . . . il curiale?

BASILIO (*stupito*)
Il curiale?

CONTE (*interrompendo, a Basilio*)

Io gli ho narrato
che già tutto è combinato.
Non è ver?

BARTOLO
Sì, tutto io so.

BASILIO

Ma, Don Bartolo, spiegatevi . . .

CONTE (*c. s., a Bartolo*)

Ehi, Dottore, una parola.
(*a Basilio*)
Don Basilio, son da voi.
(*a Bartolo*)
Ascoltate un poco qua.
(Fate un po' ch'ei vada via,
ch'ei ci scopra ho gran timore:
della lettera, signore,
ei l'affare ancor non sa.)

BARTOLO

(Dite bene, mio signore;
or lo mando via di qua.)

ROSINA

(Io mi sento il cor tremar!)

FIGARO

(Non vi state a distubar.)

BASILIO

(Ah, qui certo v'é un pasticcio;
non s'arriva a indovinar.)

CONTE (*a Basilio*)

Colla febbre, Don Basilio,
chi v'insegna a passeggiar?

BASILIO (*stupito*)

Colla febbre?

CONTE

E che vi pare?
Siete giallo come un morto.

BASILIO

Sono giallo come un morto?

FIGARO
(*tastando il polso a Basilio*)

Bagattella!
Cospetton! Che tremarella!
Questa è febbre scarlattina!

BASILIO

Scarlattina!

CONTE

(*dà a Basilio una borsa di soppiatto.*)
Via, prendete medicina,
non vi state a rovinar.

FIGARO

Presto, presto , andate a letto.

CONTE

Voi paura inver mi fate.

ROSINA

Dice bene, andate a letto.

FIGARO

(to Bartolo and interrupting him)

And now what is it?
Are you paying me to shave you
Or to listen to you talk?
How am I supposed to shave you
If you choose to take a walk?

BARTOLO (to Figaro)

I am coming. Just a moment.
            (to Basilio)
You saw the lawyer?

BASILIO (astonished)

Saw the lawyer?

COUNT (to Basilio)

I told him all arrangements have been
    made already.
(to Bartolo) Did I not?

BARTOLO

Yes, yes, yes, you did. Yes, you did.

BASILIO

Doctor Bartolo, explain to me . . .

COUNT (interrupting)

Doctor, I must tell you something,
Something secret and important.

(turning to Basilio)

Don Basilio, just a moment.
            (turning to Bartolo)
There are things I must explain,
But in private.
            (confidentially)
Don't let Don Basilio hear you,
Or he may upset your planning.

ROSINA (aside)

I could almost die of fright.

FIGARO (softly to Rosina)

Ev'rything will be all right.

COUNT (aside, to Bartolo)

He knows nothing of the letter,
Nothing of the whole affair.

BASILIO (to himself)

There's some underhanded dealing,
Something foul, I don't know where.

BARTOLO (to the Count)

You are right, it would be better.
We must get him out of here.

COUNT (to Basilio, aloud)

With that fever, Don Basilio,
Tell me how you dare to go about so
    freely.

BASILIO (astonished)

With a fever?

COUNT

You haven't noticed?
You are paler than a mummy.

BASILIO (astonished)

So I'm paler than a mummy.

FIGARO
(feeling Basilio's pulse)

You are trembling. And your pulse,
How it is racing,
Hundred twenty, hundred forty,
Hundred sixty, hundred eighty,
It's a case of scarlatina.

BASILIO

Scarlatina!

COUNT

(surreptitiously giving Basilio a purse)
What you need is some good tonic,
This one here is most effective
And works wonders as a cure.

FIGARO

Hurry, hurry, off to bed now.

COUNT

Your condition's very serious.

ROSINA

You may even be delirious.

BARTOLO

Presto, andate a riposar

TUTTI

Presto, andate a riposar.

BASILIO (*stupito*)

(Una borsa! . . . Andate a letto! . . .
Ma che tutti sian d'accordo!)

FIGARO

Presto a letto.

TUTTI

Presto a letto.

BASILIO

Eh, non son sordo.
Non mi faccio più pregar.

FIGARO

Che color!

CONTE

Che brutta cera!

BASILIO

Brutta cera?

CONTE, FIGARO, BARTOLO

Oh, brutta assai!

BASILIO

Dunque vado . . .

ROSINA, CONTE, FIGARO, BARTOLO

Vado, vado!
Buona sera, mio signore,
presto andate via di qua.

BASILIO

Buona sera, ben di core,
poi domani si parlerà.

ROSINA, FIGARO

Maledetto seccatore!
Pace, sonno e sanità.

ROSINA, CONTE

Buona sera, mio signore,
Pace, sono e sanità.

FIGARO, BARTOLO

Presto, presto, andate via
presto andate via di qua.

TUTTI

Presto, presto, andate via
Presto andate via di qua.

FIGARO

Orsù, signor Don Bartolo.

BARTOLO

Son qua.

(*Bartolo siede, Figaro gli cinge al collo
un asciugatoio di sponendosi a fargli
la barba; durante l'operazione Figaro
va coprendo i due amanti.*)

Stringi, bravissimo.

CONTE

Rosina, deh, ascoltatemi.

ROSINA

V'ascolto;
eccomi qua.

(*Siedono fingendo studiar musica.*)

BARTOLO

Bed rest is the only cure.

BARTOLO, ROSINA, FIGARO, COUNT

Yes, it is the only cure.

BASILIO (*astonished*)

A purse with money! And off to bed
now?
I can see that they are all in this together.

FIGARO

Off to bed now, hurry, hurry.

ROSINA, COUNT, FIGARO, BARTOLO

Off to bed now, get some re—

BASILIO (*interrupting, shouting*)

I am not deaf yet!
I am going and will do as you request.

FIGARO

You look dreadful.

COUNT

Yes, you look awful.

BASILIO

I look awful?

COUNT, FIGARO, BARTOLO

Yes, simply ghastly.

BASILIO (*resolutely*)

I am going.

ROSINA, COUNT, FIGARO, BARTOLO

Bravo!
Till tomorrow, Don Basilio.
Hurry home and get some rest.

BASILIO

Till tomorrow, ev'rybody.
Then again I'll be your guest.

ROSINA, FIGARO

Was there ever, was there ever
Such a stubborn pest!

ROSINA, COUNT

Till tomorrow, Don Basilio.
Hurry home and take a rest.

FIGARO, BARTOLO

Till tomorrow, Don Basilio.
What you need is a good rest.

ROSINA, COUNT, FIGARO, BARTOLO

Hurry home and take a rest.
(*They chase Basilio out.*)

BASILIO (*returning*)

Till tomorrow, till tomorrow.

ALL THE OTHERS
(*chasing Basilio out again*)

Till tomorrow, Don Basilio.
Hurry home and take a rest.

FIGARO

Come on, Doctor Bartolo.

BARTOLO

All right, I'm here.
(*Bartolo sits down again. Figaro ties a
a napkin around his neck before
shaving him and stands so as to hide
the lovers.*)

Pull harder! That's excellent.

COUNT
(*sitting beside Rosina at the piano*)

Rosina, dear, listen carefully.

ROSINA

I hear you, I hear you.
Speak, dearest love.
(*They pretend to be studying the
music.*)

CONTE (*a Rosina, con cautela*)

A mezzanotte in punto
a prendervi qui siamo:
or che la chiave abbiamo
non v'è da dubitar.

FIGARO (*distraendo Bartolo*)

Ahi! . . . ahi! . . .

BARTOLO

Che cos'è stato? . . .

FIGARO

Un non so che nell'occhio!
Guardate . . .
non toccate . . .
soffiate per pietà.

ROSINA

A mezzanotte in punto,
anima mia, t'aspetto.
Io già l'istante affretto
che a te mi stringerà.

CONTE

Ora avvertir vi voglio,

(*Bartolo si alza e si avvicina agli
amanti.*)

cara, che il vostro foglio,
perchè non fosse inutile
il mio travestimento . . .

BARTOLO (*scattando*)

Il suo travestimento?
Ah, ah! bravi, bravissimi!
Sor Alonso, bravo! bravi!
Bricconi, birbanti!
Ah, voi tutti quanti
avete giurato
di farmi crepar!
Su, fuori, furfanti,
vi voglio accoppar.
Di rabbia, di sdegno
mi sento crepar.

ROSINA, CONTE e FIGARO

La testa vi gira.
Ma zitto, Dottore,
vi fate burlar.
Tacete, tacete,
non serve gridar.
(Intesi già siamo,
non vo' replicar.)
(*Partono, meno Bartolo.*)

BARTOLO

Ah! disgraziato me! ma come? ed io
non mi accorsi di nulla! Ah! Don
Basilio sa certo qualche cosa. Ehi! chi
   è di là?
Chi è di là?
(*Comparisce Ambrogio.*)
Senti, Ambrogio:
corri da Don Basilio qui rimpetto,
digli ch'io qua l'aspetto,
che venga immantinente,
che ho gran cose da dirgli, e ch'io non
   vado
perchè . . . perchè . . . perchè ho di
   gran ragioni.
Va subito.
(*Ambrogio parte ed entra Berta.*)
(*a Berta*)
Di guardia
tu piantati alla porta, e poi . . . no, no .
(Non me ne fido) Io stesso ci starò.

(*Parte.*)

No. 16

Recitativo ed Aria

BERTA

Che vecchio sospettoso! Vada pure
e ci stia finchè crepa . . .
Sempre gridi e tumulti in questa casa:

COUNT

We'll come for you at midnight
And leave this house forever.
Don Bartolo will never find out
Till we are gone.

FIGARO

(*trying to distract Bartolo*)

Ow! Ow!

BARTOLO

What is the matter?

FIGARO

It is my eye,
I think there's something in it.
You see it? Do not touch it,
Just blow it, it will come out alone.
(*Bartolo busies himself with Figaro's eye.*)

ROSINA (*softly to the Count*)

At midnight I'll be waiting,
Happy and so excited.
At last we'll be united,
My dearest love, my own.

COUNT

Dearest, I think I'd better
Inform you that your letter . . .
In order to succeed this time,
Disguised as Don Alonso . . .

BARTOLO

(*has overheard the Count; he gets out of his chair and walks toward the lovers*)

Disguised as Don Alonso? Aha!
You lying hypocrites!
Don Alonso! Bravo, bravo!
You scoundrels! You swindlers!
You bandits! You traitors! You wretches!
You think you can cheat me,
Confuse and mistreat me,
Abuse and torment me
Until I am dead!
But now you won't trick me.
Get out of here quickly
Before I get violent and blood will be shed!

ROSINA, COUNT, FIGARO

Don't get so excited.
Stop ranting and raving,
Stop screaming and shouting.
No more misbehaving
Or people will think you are losing your head.
Be quiet, be silent.
O doctor, be silent,
Enough has been said.
(*to each other*)
We'll tease him a little,
We're winning the battle.
(*to Bartolo*)
You're losing your head.
Don't shout, don't shout,
You're losing your head.

BARTOLO

Get out, get out,
Or blood will be shed!
(*All leave, except Bartolo*)

BARTOLO (*alone*)

Ah, what an awful day! What is this?
I don't know what to think. Ah, Don Basilio knows more than he lets on.
(*calls*) Bertha! Ambrosius!
(*They appear.*)

BARTOLO (*to Ambrosius*)

Run as fast as you can to Don Basilio. Tell him that I must see him, and tell him to hurry. It's of greatest importance. I cannot leave here because . . . because . . . never mind, just go and tell him. Away with you! (*to Bertha*) You, Bertha, you stay right by the doorway and call me . . . No, no (*aside*) I cannot trust her. I'll watch the door myself. (*He leaves the room.*)

No. 16

Recitative and Aria

BERTHA

My master is a monster. I have loved him, but from now on I despise him! Ev'ry moment he is screaming at

litiga, si piange, si minaccia . . . Sì,
Non v'è un'ora di pace
con questo vecchio avaro e brontolone!
Oh, che casa! Oh, che casa in confu-
    sione!
Il vecchiotto cerca moglie,
vuol marito la ragazza;
quello freme, questa è pazza,
tutti e due son da legar.
Ma che cosa è questo amore
che fa tutti delirar?
Egli è un male universale,
una smania, un pizzicore,
un solletico, un tormento . . .
Poverina, anch'io lo sento,
nè so come finirà.
Oh! vecchiaia maledetta!
Son da tutti disprezzata,
E vecchietta disperata.
mi convien così crepar.

(*Parte.*)

ATTO TERZO

*Camera con griglia come nel primo
atto. Bartolo e Don Basilio.*

BARTOLO

(*introducendo Don Basilio*)

Dunque voi Don Alonso
non conoscete affatto?

BASILIO

Affatto.

BARTOLO

Ah, certo il Conte lo mandò.
Qualche gran tradimento si
    prepara.

BASILIO

Io poi dico che quell'amico
era il Conte in persona.

BARTOLO

Il Conte?

BASILIO

Il Conte.
(La borsa parla chiaro.)

BARTOLO

Sia chi si vuole . . . amico, dal notaro
vo' in questo punto andare; in questa
    sera
stipular di mie nozze io vo' il contratto.

BASILIO

Il notar? siete matto?
Piove a torrenti, e poi,
questa sera il notaro
è impegnato con Figaro; il barbiere
marita sua nipote.

BARTOLO

Una nipote?
Che nipote? Il barbiere
non ha nipoti. Ah, qui v'è qualche
    imbroglio.
Questa notte i bricconi
me la vogliono far; presto, il notaro
qua venga sull'istante.
(*Gli dà una chiave.*)
Ecco la chiave del portone: andate,
presto, per carità.

BASILIO

Non temete; in due salti io torno qua.

(*Parte.*)

BARTOLO

Per forza o per amore
Rosina avrà da cedere. Cospetto!
Mi viene un'altra idea. Questo biglietto
(*Cava dalla tasca il biglietto datogli
    dal Conte.*)
che scrisse la ragazza ad Almaviva
potria servir . . . che colpo da maestro!

Rosina. What arguments and quarrels! It's disgusting. Oh, what I have to put up with, with such an old and nasty grouch of a master! It unnerves me. I'm afraid there'll be a disaster!

When old men wish to be married
And young women long for husbands,
Both are frenzied, both are harried.
They completely lose their mind.
Yes, yes, they completely lose their mind.
They're confused and they are blind.
What has made them both so frantic,
This disease they're speaking of?
What makes old and young romantic?
What's this illness they call love?
It's a dreadful epidemic,
It's a universal mania,
It's a stinging, wild desire,
It's an all-consuming fire.
I myself can feel it burning,
My poor heart is sick with yearning,
And it makes me want to cry.
I'm a spinster and I'm aging,
How could I attract a lover?
Not engaged and not engaging,
I'm so lonely I could die!
Yes, yes, I'd better off to die.
I am neither young nor pretty,
No one wants me for a wife.
What a shame and what a pity,
What a rotten, rotten life!

(*She leaves.*)

ACT THREE

The same room with barred windows, as in Act I.

BARTOLO
(*ushering in Basilio*)

Are you trying to tell me you don't know Don Alonso?

BASILIO

Precisely.

BARTOLO

In that case he's a spy of the Count's. Some enormous deceit is in the making.

BASILIO

And I say, this Don Alonso is none other than the Count.

BARTOLO

You think so?

BASILIO

I know so. (*to himself*) His money said so, clearly.

BARTOLO

So much the worse. There's only one way out. I'll go and get the lawyer. This very evening he must draw up the papers for my marriage.

BASILIO

Tonight? Are you crazy? It's raining buckets, and further, I found out that the lawyer has some dealings with Figaro. I am told his niece is to be married.

BARTOLO

What are you saying? What niece? That is nonsense, he has no niece. To me that sounds suspicious. Those two rascals are together in some gigantic hoax. Listen, Don Basilio, you go and get the lawyer. Here is the key to the front door.
(*gives him a key*)
See that you hurry, all is at stake!

BASILIO

Don't you worry, in a flash I shall be back. (*He leaves.*)

BARTOLO

This evening we shall be married, or my name is not Don Bartolo . . . I have it! I just got an idea!
(*From his pocket he takes the letter given him by the Count.*)
If with the letter Rosina wrote today to Count Almaviva, I could convince her . . . oh, what a stroke of genius! Don Alonso, I will show you

Don Alonso, il briccone,
senza volerlo mi diè l'armi in mano.
Ehi, Rosina, Rosina, avanti, avanti;
(*Rosina dalle sue camere entra senza
    parlare.*)
del vostro amante io vi vo' dar novella.
Povera sciagurata! In verità
collocaste assai bene il vostro affetto!
Del vostro amor sappiate
ch'ei si fa giuoco in sen d'un'altra
    amante.
Ecco la prova.
(*Le dà il biglietto.*)

ROSINA

Oh cielo! il mio biglietto!

BARTOLO

Don Alonso e il barbiere
congiuran contro voi; non vi fidate.
Nelle braccia del Conte d'Almaviva
vi vogliono condurre.

ROSINA

(In braccio a un altro!
Che mai sento! . . . ah, Lindoro!
    ah, traditore!
Ah sì! . . . vendetta! e vegga,
vegga quell'empio chi è Rosina.)
Dite . . . signore, di sposarmi
voi bramavate . . .

BARTOLO

E il voglio.

ROSINA

Ebben, si faccia!
Io . . . son contena! ma all'istante.
    Udite:
a mezzanotte qui sarà l'indegno
con Figaro il barbier; con lui fuggire
per sposarlo io voleva.

BARTOLO

Ah, scellerati!
Corro a sbarrar la porta.

ROSINA

Ah, mio signore!
Entran per la finestra. Hanno la chiave.

BARTOLO

Non mi muovo di qui.
Ma . . . e se fossero armati? Figlia mia,
poichè tu sei sì bene illuminata,
facciam così. Chiuditi a chiave in
    camera,
io vo' a chiamar la forza;
dirò che son due ladri, e come tali,
corpo di Bacco! l'avremo da vedere!
Figlia, chiuditi presto; io vado via.

(*Parte.*)

ROSINA

Quanto, quanto è crudel la sorte mia!

(*Parte.*)

No. 17
Temporale

(*Scoppia un temporale. Dalla finestra
di prospetto si vedono frequenti lam-
pi, e si sente il rumore del tuono.
Sulla fine del temporale si vede dal
di fuori aprirsi la gelosia, ed entrano
uno dopo l'altro Figaro ed il Conte
avvolti in mantelli e bagnati dalla
pioggia. Figaro avrà in mano una
lanterna accesa.*)

No. 18
Recitativo e Terzetto

FIGARO

Alfine, eccoci qua.

CONTE

Figaro, dammi man. Poter del mondo!
Che tempo indiavolato!

FIGARO

Tempo da innamorati.

CONTE

Ehi, fammi lume.
    (*Figaro accende i lumi.*)
Dove sarà Rosina?

FIGARO (*spiando*)

Ora vedremo . . .
Eccola appunto.

how I will use the letter you have brought me! Hey, Rosina, Rosina, where are you?

(*Rosina comes from her room.*)

Come quickly, I want to give you most important information. How could you be so foolish! I am afraid you have wasted your love upon an impostor. He who pretends to love you is trying to trick you. He loves another woman. (*gives the letter to Rosina*) Here is the proof.

ROSINA

My letter! How did you get it?

BARTOLO

Don Alonso and the barber are plotting to deceive you and to betray you. They are scheming to buy you for their master, the Count Almaviva.

ROSINA (*to herself*)

Count Almaviva! How revolting! O, Lindoro, how could you do this? But now I'll show you, you villain! I will take vengeance for your betrayal. (*to Bartolo*) Tell me, dear guardian, do you still wish to become my husband?

BARTOLO

I should say so!

ROSINA

All right, so be it. Take me, I am willing. But right away. Now listen. Tonight at midnight he will come to get me, aided by the barber. I had intended to elope with Don Alonso.

BASILIO

Treacherous villains! The door must be firmly locked.

ROSINA

That will be useless. They're entering by the balcony. They have the key.

BARTOLO

I won't move from the spot! But just suppose they have weapons? Little girlie, because you are displaying such good judgment, here is my plan. Stay in your room and lock it and I shall call the police. I'll tell them they are swindlers. They shall be punished. Leave it to me. We'll send them straight to prison. Now, dear, do as I ask you. I must be going.

ROSINA

Lindoro, what have you done to your Rosina! (*They leave.*)

No. 17

Storm

From the windows frequent flashes of lightning are seen; thunder is heard. When the storm subsides the shutters are opened from without. Figaro, followed by the Count, enters by the window. They are both wrapped in cloaks; Figaro carries a lantern.)

No. 18

Recitative and Trio

FIGARO

At last, sir, we have arrived.

COUNT

Figaro, lend me a hand. That was some weather! It's only fit for devils!

FIGARO

Also for eloping lovers.

COUNT

Here, raise your lantern.
        (*Figaro does so.*)
Where is my dear Rosina?

FIGARO (*looking around*)

She must be waiting. Ah, there she comes.

CONTE (*con trasporto*)

Ah, mio tesoro!

ROSINA (*respingendolo*)

Indietro,
anima scellerata; io qui di mia
stolta credulità venni soltanto
a riparar lo scorno, a dimostrarti
qual sono, e quale amante
perdesti, anima indegna e sconoscente!

CONTE (*sorpreso*)

Io son di sasso.

FIGARO (*sorpreso*)

Io non capisco niente.

CONTE

Ma per pietà . . .

ROSINA

Taci. Fingesti amore
per vendermi alle voglie
di quel tuo vil Conte Almaviva . . .

CONTE (*con gioia*)

Al Conte?
Ah, sei delusa! . . . oh, me felice! . . .
  adunque
tu di verace amore
ami Lindor? Rispondi!

ROSINA

Ah, sì! T'amai purtroppo!

CONTE

Ah, non è tempo
di più celarsi, anima mia; ravvisa
(*S'inginocchia gettando il mantello che
  viene raccolto da Figaro.*)
colui che sì gran tempo
seguì tue traccie, che per te sospira,
che sua ti vuole; mira, o mio tesoro,
Almaviva son io, non son Lindoro.

ROSINA (*stupefatta, con gioia*)

(Ah! qual colpo inaspettato!
Egli stesso? o Ciel, che sento!
Di sorpresa e di contento
son vicina a delirar.)

FIGARO

(Son rimasti senza fiato:
ora muoion di contento.
Guarda, guarda il mio talento
che bel colpo seppe far!)

CONTE

(Qual trionfo inaspettato!
Me felice! oh bel momento!
Ah! d'amore e di contento
son vicino a delirar.)

ROSINA

Mio signor! . . . ma voi . . . ma io . . .

CONTE

Ah, non più, non più, ben mio.
Il bel nome di mia sposa,
idol mio, t'attende già.

ROSINA

Il bel nome di tua sposa,
oh, qual gioia al cor mi dà!

CONTE

Sei contenta?

ROSINA

Ah! mio signore!

ROSINA e CONTE

Dolce nodo.

FIGARO (*contraffacendo*)

(Nodo!)

ROSINA e CONTE

. . . avventurato
che fai paghi . . .

FIGARO

Andiamo!

COUNT (*transported*)

O my darling!

ROSINA (*repelling him*)

Away! I do not want to see you! The only reason why I am here is to reject you, to tell you what I think of you, and express my contempt so that you know that you lost me. Faithless deceiver! Shameless pretender!

COUNT

This is a nightmare!

FIGARO

I'm absolutely speechless!

COUNT

But dearest love . . .

ROSINA

Traitor! You want to sell me, pretending that you loved me, to your vile lord and master, Count Almaviva!

COUNT

You darling! Blessed deception! Oh, happy moment! Tell me, then it is to Lindoro you gave your heart? Speak freely!

ROSINA

I did, I loved you dearly.

COUNT

Ah, then it is high time that you should know your future husband.

(*He kneels before her, throwing off his cloak, revealing himself, richly dressed. Figaro picks up the cloak.*)

Forgive me, I am your fond admirer, he who so long has ardently pursued you with growing passion. Love was my only motive. I'm no longer Lindoro, I'm Almaviva.

ROSINA

Ah, how glorious!
What a joyous happy ending!
Almaviva, the Count, my lover.
With what wonder I now discover!
I'm so happy that I could die!

FIGARO (*to himself*)

Unexpected happy ending,
Now she knows who is her lover,
When my genius I uncover,
What a mastermind am I!

COUNT

Ah, how joyous!
What a truly happy ending!
How delightful to be her lover.
All life's glory we shall discover.
What a happy man am I!

ROSINA

Ah, my lord . . . but . . . you are so noble . . .

COUNT

Not "my lord." Do not call me by that title.
I entreat you, call me "husband."
That's the title I adore.

ROSINA

Call you "husband." Ah, how lovely!
Nothing else would please me more.

COUNT

Are you happy?

ROSINA

Dearest beloved, my dearest husband!
Oh how glorious . . .

FIGARO (*imitating comically*)

Glorious . . .

ROSINA

To be united, no more ruses,

FIGARO (*aside*)

Let's hurry.

ROSINA

. . . i miei desiri!

CONTE

Hai veduto due persone?

ROSINA e CONTE

Dolce nodo . . .

FIGARO

Sì, signore.

FIGARO

Nodo . . . Presto andiamo.

ROSINA, CONTE e FIGARO

Che si fa?

ROSINA e CONTE

. . . avventurato
che fai paghi.

ROSINA

Zitti, zitti, piano, piano,
non facciamo confusione;
per la scala del balcone
presto andiamo via di qua.

FIGARO

(paghi) Vi sbrigate.

ROSINA e CONTE

Alla fin de' miei martiri
tu sentisti, amor, pietà.

CONTE

Zitti, zitti, piano, piano,
non facciamo confusione;
per la scala del balcone
presto andiamo via di qua.

FIGARO

Presto andiamo, vi sbrigate;
via, lasciate quei sospiri.
Se si tarda, i miei raggiri
fanno fiasco in verità.
(guardando fuori del belcone)
Ah! cospetto! che ho veduto!
Alla porta una lanterna . . .
due persone! . . . che si fa?

FIGARO

Zitti, zitti, piano, piano,
non facciamo confusione;
per la scala del balcone
presto andiamo via di qua.
(con angoscia)

ROSINA

And no more grieving.

COUNT

Ah, how glorious . . .

FIGARO (*imitating comically*)

Glorious . . .

COUNT

To be united . . .

FIGARO (*urging*)

Finish, I beg of you.

COUNT

No more ruses . . .

FIGARO (*imitating*)

Ruses . . .

COUNT

No more deceit.

FIGARO

We must hurry.

ROSINA AND COUNT

This is joy beyond believing.
Love is kindly, love is sweet.

FIGARO

Not a moment of blissful sighs
  and swooning.
It is high time we were leaving,
Or we still may meet defeat.
Hurry up, for heaven's sake!

COUNT AND ROSINA

Love is kindly, love is sweet.

FIGARO

No more billing, no more cooing,
It is getting very late.
Come, come, hurry, hurry!

ROSINA AND COUNT

You are my love . . .

FIGARO (*interrupting*)

Ah, good heavens, did you see that?
Below there, near the doorway,
I see a lantern, and two people
Coming nearer. What to do?

COUNT

You have seen them . . .

FIGARO

At the door!

COUNT

Coming nearer?

FIGARO

Yes, my lord.

COUNT

They have a lantern?

FIGARO

At the doorway, right outside there
At the door!

ALL THREE

What to do?

COUNT

Hurry, scurry, hurry, scurry,
Without noise or clitter-clatter,
Out the window, down the ladder.
Be as quiet as a mouse.

ROSINA

Hurry, scurry, hurry, scurry,
While your heart goes pitter-patter.
Out the window, down the ladder.
Let us quickly leave this house.

FIGARO

Hurry, scurry, hurry, scurry,
Without noise or clitter-clatter,
Out the window, down the ladder.
Let us quickly leave this house.

(*They are about to go.*)

FIGARO

Ah, disgraziati noi! come si fa?

CONTE

Che avvenue mai?

FIGARO

La scala . . .

CONTE

Ebben?

FIGARO

La scala non v'è più.

CONTE (*sorpreso*)

Che dici?

FIGARO

Chi mai l'avrà levata?

CONTE

Quale inciampo crudel!

ROSINA

Me sventurata!

FIGARO

Zi . . . zitti . . . sento gente. Ora ci
    siamo.
Signor mio, che si fa?

CONTE

Mia Rosina, coraggio.
(*Si avvolge nel mantello.*)

FIGARO

Eccoli qua.
(*Si ritirano verso una delle quinte.*)
Don Basilio con lanterna in mano, in-
    troducendo un Notaio con carte.

BASILIO

(*chiamando alla quinta opposta*)
Don Bartolo! Don Bartolo!

FIGARO (*accennando al Conte*)

Don Basilio.

CONTE

E quell'altro?

FIGARO

Ve', ve', il nostro notaro. Allegramente.
Lasciate fare a me. Signor Notaro:
(*Basilio e il Notaro si rivolgono e re-*
    stano sorpresi. Il Notaro si avvicina
    a Figaro.)
dovevate in mia casa
stipular questa sera
il contratto di nozze
fra il conte d'Almavi· ι e mia nipote.
Gli sposi, eccoli qua.. vete indosso
la scrittura?
(*Il Notaio cava la scrittura.*)
Benissimo.

BASILIO

Ma piano.
Don Bartolo . . . dov'è?

CONTE

(*chiamando a parte Basilio, cavandosi*
    un anello dal dito, e additandogli di
    tacere)
Ehi, Don Basilio,
quest'anello è per voi.

BASILIO

Ma io . . .

CONTE (*cavando una pistola*)

Per voi
vi sono ancor due palle nel cervello
se v'opponete.

BASILIO (*prende l'anello.*)

Oibò, prendo l'anello.
Chi firma?

CONTE

Eccoci qua.
(*Sottoscrivono.*)

CONTE

Son testimoni
Figaro e Don Basilio. Essa è mia sposa.

FIGARO

Evviva!

CONTE

Oh, mio contento!

FIGARO (*at the window*)

Ah, what a dreadful blow, what shall we do?

COUNT

What is the matter?

FIGARO

The ladder . . .

COUNT

Well, what?

FIGARO

It is no longer there!

COUNT

The ladder?

FIGARO

But who could have removed it?

COUNT

Someone tricked us; we're trapped!

ROSINA

Oh, how disastrous!

FIGARO

One moment, I hear people. We are discovered. I'm afraid it looks bad.

COUNT
(*wraps himself in his cloak*)

Dear Rosina, I'll protect you!

FIGARO

Let them come in.
(*They retire to the side.*)

BASILIO
(*accompanied by a notary, calling*)

Don Bartolo, Don Bartolo!

FIGARO (*softly, to the Count*)

It's Basilio

COUNT (*whispering*)

Who is with him?

FIGARO

My, my, he came with the lawyer. What could be better! I'll carry on from here. (*comes forward*) How do you do, sir. As you know, I have summoned you this evening to my house to perform the marriage between Count Almaviva and a young lady. The couple happens to be here. I hope you brought the papers with you?
(*The notary takes out a document.*)
That's excellent.

BASILIO

One moment, Don Bartolo's not here.

COUNT
(*takes Basilio aside and draws a ring from his finger*)

Hey, Don Basilio, here's a diamond for your trouble.

BASILIO

Beg pardon . . .

COUNT
(*pointing a pistol at Basilio*)

Or else, if you prefer, a bullet through your forehead. One or the other.

BASILIO

I see. I'll take the diamond.
(*takes the ring*)
Your servant.

COUNT (*signing*)

Now we can sign You are one witness; Figaro will be the other. On with the signing!

FIGARO (*signs*)

We've done it!

COUNT

What a glorious moment!

ROSINA

Oh, sospirata mia felicità!

FIGARO

Evviva!
(*Nell'atto che il Conte bacia la mano a
Rosina, Figaro abbracia goffamente
Basilio, ed entrano Don Bartolo e
(un Uffiziale con soldati.*)

BARTOLO

(*additando Figaro ed il Conte e slanci-
andosi contro Figaro.*)

Fermi tutti. Eccoli qua.

FIGARO

Colle buone, signor.

BARTOLO

Signor, son ladri.
Arrestate, arrestate.

UFFIZIALE

Mio signore.
il suo nome?

CONTE

Il mio nome
è quel d'un uomo d'onore. Lo sposo io
son di questa . . .

BARTOLO

Eh, andate al diavolo! Rosina esser
deve mia sposa: non è vero?

ROSINA

Io sua sposa? Oh, nemmeno per
pensiero.

BARTOLO

Come? Come, fraschetta?
(*additando il Conte*)
Arrestate, vi dico,
è un ladro.

FIGARO

Or, or l'accoppo.

BARTOLO

È un furfante, è un briccon!

UFFIZIALE (*al Conte*)

Signore . . .

CONTE

Indietro!

UFFIZIALE (*con impazienza*)

Il nome?

CONTE

Indietro, dico,
indietro . . .

UFFIZIALE

Ehi, mio signor! basso quel tono.
Chi è lei?

CONTE

Il Conte d'Almaviva io sono.

No. 19

Scena ed Aria.

BARTOLO

Il Conte! Ah, che mai sento!
Ma cospetto!

CONTE

T'accheta, invan t'adopri,
resisti invan. De' tuoi rigori insani
giunse l'ultimo istante. In faccia al
mondo io dichiaro altamente costei mia
   sposa.
(*a Rosina*)
Il nostro nodo, o cara.
opra è d'amore. Amore che ti fe' mia
   consorte,
Respira omai: del fido sposo in
   braccio,
vieni, vieni a goder sorte più lieta.

BARTOLO

Ma io . . .

CONTE

Taci . . .

ROSINA (*signs*)

Oh, what a happy ending to all my grief!

FIGARO

Stupendous!

(*As the Count kisses Rosina's hand and Figaro grotesquely embraces Basilio, Don Bartolo enters with an officer and a patrol of soldiers.*)

BARTOLO

No one move! Stay where you are!
(*pointing to Figaro and the Count*)

FIGARO

Give me time to explain.

BARTOLO (*to the officer*)

At last we caught them. Do your duty and arrest them.

OFFICER

Will the gentleman give his name?

COUNT

For the moment, I'll say my name is a good one. This lady here is my wife.

BARTOLO

I say to hell with him!
Rosina, you have promised to marry me, have you not?

ROSINA

I should marry you? I would rather die a spinster.

BARTOLO

Would you? You little viper!
(*to the officer and pointing to the Count*)
Take this man here to prison, he's a swindler!

FIGARO

I'd like to choke him!

BARTOLO

He's a robber, he's a thief!

OFFICER (*to the Count*)

Your name, sir.

COUNT

Keep quiet!

OFFICER (*impatiently*)

Your name, sir?

COUNT

You, hold your tongue. Attention!

OFFICER

Hey, my good man, you will repent this. Who are you?

COUNT

I am Count Almaviva in person.

No. 19

*Scene

BARTOLO

Good heavens, Count Almaviva!
Devil take it!

COUNT

Be quiet ,no more resisting. It would be vain. At last we see the end of your cruel persecutions. Before the world I proclaim Rosina my wife, my countess. It's true love only that binds our hearts together, a bond no power can sever. A love that will endure now and forever. Come, my beloved, you have attained your freedom. Dearest, let us depart now, happiness beckons.

BARTOLO (*protesting*)

Your lordship . . .

COUNT

Silence!

*This scene until No. 20 is customarily omitted in stage performances.

BASILIO

Ma voi . . .

CONTE

Olà, t'accheta.

Cessa di più resistere,
non cimentar mio sdegno.
Spezzato è il giogo indegno
di tanta crudeltà.
Della beltà dolente,
d'un innocente amore
l'avaro tuo furore
più non trionferà.
E tu, infelice vittima
d'un reo poter tiranno,
sottratta al giogo barbaro,
cangia in piacer l'affanno
e in sen d'un fido sposo
gioisci in libertà.
Cari amici . . .

CORO

Non temete.

CONTE

Questo nodo . . .

CORO

Non si scioglie,
sempre a lei vi stringerà.

CONTE

Ah, il più lieto, il più felice
è il mio cor de' cori amanti;
non fuggite, o lieti istanti
della ma felicità.

CORO

Annodar due cori amanti
è piacer che egual non ha.

No. 20

Recitativo e Finale II

BARTOLO

Insomma, io ho tutti i torti!

FIGARO

Eh, purtroppo è così!

BARTOLO (*a Basilio*)

Ma tu, briccone,
tu pur tradirmi e far da testimonio!

BASILIO

Ah, Don Bartolo mio, quel signor
    Conte
certe ragioni ha in tasca,
certi argomenti a cui non si risponde.

BARTOLO

Ed io, bestia solenne,
per meglio assicurare il matrimonio,
portai via la scala del balcone.

FIGARO

Ecco che fa un'INUTIL PRECAU-
ZIONE.

BARTOLO

Ma . . . e la dote? io non posso . . .

CONTE

Eh via; di dote
io bisogno non ho: va; te la dono.

FIGARO

Ah, ah! ridete adesso?
Bravissimo, Don Bartolo,
ho veduto alla fin rasserenarsi
quel vostro ceffo amaro e furibondo.
Eh, i bricconi han fortuna in questo
    mondo.

ROSINA

Dunque, signor Don Bartolo?

BASILIO

Your lordship . . .

COUNT

You both, be quiet.

(to Bartolo)

Better surrender gacefully,
Before I lose my patience.
Your days of domination
Are over now and past.
You cannot rule Rosina,
Torture her or torment her,
Nor greedily prevent her
From finding love at last.
Your greed cannot prevent
This gentle heart
From finding love at last.

(to Rosina)

And you, so sadly trapped
Within the toils of a tyrant's power,
Will know the glow of happiness.
Your life will bloom and flower.
Your faithful love beside you,
Your future will be bright.

(to the others)

Dear companions, I am grateful . . .

CHORUS OF THE GUARD

We all wish you joy forever,
Days of sweetness and contentment,
Years of pleasure and delight.

COUNT

I have never been so happy,
How this love of mine delights me.
May this rapture that excites me
Never leave my joyful heart.

CHORUS OF THE GUARD

As the future beckons brightly,
They unite, no more to part.

No. 20
Recitative and Finale II

BARTOLO

I see now, clearly, I was a fool.

FIGARO

Yes, that is so, I'm afraid.

BARTOLO *(to Basilio)*

But you, you scoundrel, you of all
people, you acted as a witness!

BASILIO

What else could I do? I could not help
it. The Count carries in his pocket
certain devices which left me no al-
ternative.

BARTOLO

And I, stupid idiot, have actually helped
them to get married by removing
the ladder from the balcony!

FIGARO

That's what I call "superfluous precaution."

BARTOLO

But, but the dowry! All the money . . .

COUNT

Don't worry, the dowry is the least of
my concerns. It's yours, you may have
it.

FIGARO

Haha! What do you say now? At last,
my dear Don Bartolo, I have lived to
see the day when it would happen
that this grouchy face of yours be-
comes all smiles. True, you have lost
your Rosina, but you've gained a
fortune.

ROSINA *(to Bartolo)*

Well, then, are you satisfied?

BARTOLO

Sì, sì, ho capito tutto.

CONTE

Ebben, dottore?

BARTOLO

Si, si, che serve? quel ch'è fatto è fatto.
Andate pur, che il ciel vi benedica.

FIGARO

Bravo, bravo, un abbraccio,
venite qua, dottore.

ROSINA

Ah, noi felici!

CONTE

Oh, fortunato amore!

FIGARO

Di sì felice innesto
serbiam memoria eterna;
io smorzo la lanterna;
qui più non ho che far.
(*Smorza la lanterna.*)

ROSINA

Costò sospiri e pene,
un sì felice istante:
alfin quest'alma amante
comincia a respirar.

TUTTI

Amore e fede eterna
si vegga in voi (noi) regnar.

FINE

BARTOLO

I am, Countess Almaviva.

COUNT

Agreed, it's settled.

BARTOLO

Yes, yes, it's settled. I get all the money, you get the girl. I give you my blessing.

FIGARO

That's the spirit! Let's shake hands, and I am still your barber.

ROSINA

Oh, I'm so happy!

COUNT

Yes, all is well that ends well.

FIGARO

Success has crowned our venture.
The lovers are united,
The flame of love is lighted.
I'll snuff the lantern light.

(*puts out his lantern*)

ROSINA, BERTHA, FIGARO, BARTOLO
COUNT BASILIO AND SOLDIERS

In love and faith forever
The happy pair unite,
And favored by good fortune
The future will be bright,
Forever bright!

END OF THE OPERA